MASTER CHINESE BUSINESS CULTURE

Becoming a China expert

Qingshun Zou

To my readers

It is with emotion that I address myself to you, the readers of my book. So much has happened in the international economic and geopolitical spheres in the last few years! And we are all living in a time of turmoil and uncertainty for the future. China is in the news every day and many Western economic and political leaders willingly share their visions and predictions about China. But their statements, frequently wrong, often provoke feelings of frustration and misunderstanding in me. I realized that the Western world, in which I live and whose culture has fascinated me for three decades, must urgently address the backwardness that impedes its attempts to understand China, its people and culture—for its own benefit as well as for China and the world.

When I arrived in Europe nearly thirty years ago, I was instantly attracted to its culture which has continuously enriched my life journey. I mainly read works in French and English; French writers such as Marc Levy, Éric-Emmanuel Schmitt and François Cheng have become my idols. I have also developed an interest in French cinema, especially the finesse of its humor and sensitivity. The discovery of psychology was another highlight in my life: Freud and Jung gave me a new understanding of our human condition, while the neurologist, psychiatrist and writer Boris Cyrulnik became my reference in the field of human science. When a friend introduced me to the works of Baruch Spinoza, a Dutch philosopher of Portuguese Sephardi origin, I realized that there were many similarities between his approach and that of the Chinese philosopher Lao Zi. Interested in religions, I browsed through the Bible, where many parables are identical to the accounts found in Chinese philosophies. Amazed by Western art, I was initiated into classical music by learning to play an instrument. My list of interests in Western culture is indeed long.

The differences and similarities between Western and Chinese culture are certainly striking. But I disagree with the assertions of some Western political leaders that China does not share their values. While following different paths, China, the West and the rest of world pursue the same values: love, peace, justice and freedom.

My total immersion in the Western world and unbridled admiration for its culture led me to neglect my native culture for many years. Today, thanks to writing this book, I have had the opportunity to revisit my native culture by measuring all of its complexity and depth. In publishing this book, I wish to convey to Westerners a new view of China and hopefully to contribute, in my capacity, to a better mutual understanding between the West and China.

Qingshun Zou
May 11, 2021

Acknowledgements

Writing this book was an unusual, solitary and rewarding journey. After receiving several publication offers from European and American publishing houses, I still decided to self-publish my work. This allows my readers to have access to my book at a favorable price and in a reasonable time frame.

I have many people to thank for their love, friendship and encouragement that gave me the strength to complete this book. I express my deepest appreciation to my friends and my family, Catherine Tapponnier, Henriette Loutan-Barde, Aline Saurer, Marianne Aerni, Raoli Wang-Cruchet, Shuhua Ge, Jian Dambach, Claire Fornerod and Sophie Fornerod.

I also extend my gratitude to Professor Philippe Laurent for his support that provided me with valuable recognition from a renowned China business expert.

My sincere thanks go to my two editors, Adeline Vanoverbeke and Colin Smith. Their professionalism and patience were precious to me. I will unhesitatingly entrust them with the editing of my second book, which is well underway.

Preface

Many similar books or articles have already been written in an attempt to explain China since it opened up to the world, especially the business world. Its numerous successes never cease to amaze or even fascinate us Westerners, all the more so as we note—with amazement and trembling (thank you Amélie Nothomb)—that they are now coming to strike a blow here. Whether it's the takeover of industrial, port, wine, hotel or cultural flagships, or the gigantic Belt and Road Initiative (BRI), nothing seems to stop their conquering appetite. Even the United States, the undisputed leader in innovation and world trade for a century, now clearly seems to be concerned about this devouring ambition, which aims to dethrone them from their imperial pedestal. Yet all this can easily be explained—and even understood—if one adopts for a moment the Chinese point of view, without compromise or bias.

This is what the author Qingshun Zou invites us to do in this book. Originally from China and with substantial experience in mainland China, she attempts to share with us her genuine passion for her native culture, as well as her understanding of our very different universe of thought. Indeed, the books or articles to which I referred in the preamble are often written by Western Sinophiles or sinologists who, despite their efforts, give us a prism of interpretation that is somewhat biased by their self-centered object of study or research. Here, it is different because Qingshun Zou is not seeking any particular academic glory, but is indeed concerned with a genuine sharing with potential readers.

She begins by describing today's China in all its political, economic, social and cultural diversity in a factual, numerical and descriptive way, without making laudatory comments and without hesitating to mention the residual weaknesses, as well as the long-standing admiration of the Chinese for the past achievements of the West. She also rightly recalls the important progress made over the last thirty years by her native country, progress that aims to ensure world leadership in sectors where it was absent until recently and, in any case, a technological autonomy favored by an ultra-fast rate of adoption of innovations by her compatriots. This is a far cry from the China that our invading ancestors knew: backward, self-sustaining and resistant to change!

Eager to make us understand what differentiates success from failure in the gigantic Chinese market, Qingshun Zou reminds us of some fundamentals and describes in detail the brilliant successes of well-known brands, whose key word is adaptability, with all the regional and local nuances to be considered in a coherent marketing plan. This logically leads the author to explain the rites and symbolism of the Chinese world, through a resurgent Confucian vision of society and gratifying historical recollection.

Etiquette as well as business meetings and meals in China are far from straightforward for newly arrived Westerners, and the author willingly takes us on a detailed tour of the mechanisms and codes, the deep meanings, while reminding us of their importance in a negotiation situation, an art in which the Chinese excel.

Long and harshly condemned during the revolutions of the 20th century since 1912, the "Confucius shop" has shown incredible resilience over time and explains so many things that at first glance seem impenetrable to us, out of pure ignorance. Indeed, we must constantly keep in mind that, in general, the Chinese often know our history and thinking better than we imagine, and in any case, much better than we know theirs.

In these circumstances, let us be humble and curious not only in approaching this instructive and practical work, but also in confronting our relationship with otherness and our view of China.

Philippe Laurent
Professor of Haute École de Gestion, Fribourg, Switzerland
April 8, 2021

Table of Contents

Introduction

"The one who knows himself and knows the other can fight a hundred battles and win a hundred victories."
—**Sun Zi,** ***The Art of War,*** **5th century BC**

This quote from the Chinese military general Sun Zi is proverbial in China. All Chinese children learn it by heart from an early age. Their parents and teachers repeat it with the aim of encouraging them to get to know others. In daily conversations, this phrase is often quoted as a reminder between people. Sun Zi was also a philosopher—his thinking plays an important role in Chinese political and economic strategies.

The Art of War was originally a book about military strategy. Its author, Sun Zi, applied triumphant strategies to win numerous battles. The book consists of 13 chapters totaling 10,000 words and runs for about 50 pages. It includes the rational analysis of the different dimensions of war and outlines the principles of intelligently pursuing a victorious war. The depth of its strategies has been revealed and examined throughout Chinese history. Studied in all military and civil schools of ancient China, Sun Zi's principles were widely applied in wars and in the management of the country, a tradition that continues in modern China. The founder of the People's Republic of China (PRC), Mao Zedong, said he used these principles to win wars against the Japanese invaders and the Chinese opposition political party Guo Ming Dang. The latter was forced to leave the Chinese mainland and took refuge in Taiwan in 1949.

The French missionary Joseph-Marie Amiot introduced *The Art of War* to the West in the 18th century. It seems that these strategies inspired Napoleon to win his battles and to conquer Europe. Today, the book is taught in military academies, universities and business schools around the world. It is cited as a reference in business, diplomatic and political think tanks. Many major Chinese and international law schools and business schools include it in their compulsory curriculum and Sun Zi's strategies have become references in the economic field.

"The one who knows himself and knows the other can fight a hundred battles and win a hundred victories" is a common translation of the original text. However, if a Chinese translated it verbatim it would be: "...one hundred battles, one hundred battles with no danger". This nuance is not insignificant; the Chinese ancestors taught that a true victory was above all to "stay alive and safe". For them, merely beating their opponents is not the priority. Chinese culture prioritizes defense and protection; it is primarily a culture of survival. Many Chinese proverbs testify to this. According to one, "If we preserved the strength of the mountain, there would be no worries about finding wood for the fire". It reflects a conservative vision of survival focused on the long term. China's iconic monument, the Great Wall, is a clear demonstration of this protective culture. For 2,000 years it has been built, destroyed and rebuilt by successive emperors of different dynasties to protect the empire from nomadic invaders coming down from the north.

"Knowing the other" is the main message emerging from this quote from Sun Zi. Today, this teaching remains rooted in Chinese culture and deeply ingrained in the Chinese people's minds. It is applied in almost all Chinese enterprises and was part of the Chinese government's strategies to reactivate economic development 40 years ago. After three decades of isolation, China began implementing profound reforms in all areas in 1978, aiming to lift its people out of poverty through strong economic growth. Relaxing the grip of state controls, the Chinese government opened its market to foreign trade and investment. Aware of the economic gap with developed countries, China immediately implemented policies that encouraged its people to get to know other nations and to be inspired by Western countries.

In 1979, French designer Pierre Cardin held a fashion show in Beijing, fascinating the Chinese public with his daring and futuristic creations. Soon after, the state leaders began to wear Western suits, leading to the overnight adoption of this style in the business world. The Chinese previously all still dressed in the Zhong Shan suit, considered by Westerners as the uniform of Maoism. In fact, the origin of the Zhong Shan suit dates back to the overthrow of the Qing dynasty in 1912, marking the abolition of imperial China. The vast majority of Chinese men of the Han ethnic group cut their braids and abandoned their robes which, until then, had been compulsory under the Qing Empire founded by the Manchu ethnic group. A new style of men's clothing, consisting of jackets and pants, was launched by political leaders advocating democracy. Adopted by students, this new outfit was named the Zhong Shan suit.

In order to communicate better with the outside world, it was essential to master foreign languages. China has placed great emphasis on education. As soon as the reform of the education system was announced in 1978, English language and European and American history were gradually imposed as the main and compulsory subjects in all secondary schools. English was very quickly integrated into elementary school. Today, the majority of students already start learning English in kindergarten. Increasing numbers of schools, especially private schools, offer French and German as complementary courses. These schools use them as their marketing campaign arguments. As a result, English language and European and

American history form part of the *Gāokǎo*, the annual national exam allowing college students to enter Chinese universities. The number of *Gāokǎo* participants reached a historical high of 10 million in 2019 (1).

Over the years, Chinese economic, diplomatic and political leaders have been striving to master English in order to improve their communication with the rest of the world. Many have mastered several Western languages and have been trained in the best American or European schools. The current Minister of Foreign Affairs, Wang Yi, speaks impeccable English. Chinese First Lady Peng Liyuan regularly delivers speeches in English on her international missions. Zhang Weiwei, professor of International Relations at Fudan University Shanghai, speaks perfect English and regularly participates in international debates on difficult topics. Chinese businessmen were usually among the students of the English faculty in their university study. For example, Jack Ma, the founder of Alibaba, has a degree in English literature and, as a former English teacher, often gives interviews in English to international media.

China's thirst for Western culture does not stop at language and history. Learning Western classical music has become a real phenomenon, constituting a promising and prosperous industry in recent decades. Today, more than 50 million Chinese study the piano in China (2) and this figure is rapidly increasing. Many children dream of playing the piano.

For some families, it is even a privilege to have a piano displayed in the living room, even if no one plays it. The number of orchestras and concert halls has exploded with the active support of the Chinese government.

In the business world, many Chinese entrepreneurs often admire Western culture. The founder of Huawei, Ren Zhengfei, is passionate about Western architecture. The company's Ox Horn Campus, located at Songshan Lake in the city of Shenzhen, is its research and development center and home to 25,000 employees. Covering 1.4 million square meters, the center comprises 108 buildings divided into 12 themes. Each group of buildings pays tribute to a European city or region: Paris (France), Verona (Italy), Césky Krumlov (Czech Republic), Freiburg (Switzerland), Heidelberg (Germany), Burgundy (France), Bologna (Italy), Windermere (UK), Luxembourg (Luxembourg), Bruges (Belgium), Oxford (UK) and Granada (Spain). The leaders of this Chinese corporate giant believe in the edifying virtues of these references and hope that they will stimulate the creativity of their employees.

To get to know others also means moving beyond the limits of your borders. Before the Covid-19 pandemic, the number of Chinese students going abroad to study was constantly increasing. In 2019, about 700,000 students left China to study abroad (3), including 370,000 that went to the United States (4). According to the latest data from Open Doors' report on international education, the United States hosted more than one million international students in the 2019–2020 academic year (5). And the U.S. Department of Commerce announced a turnover of USD 44 billion realized on this number of students (6), which means that Chinese households have invested more than USD 16 billion to send their children to the United States to study and immerse themselves in Western and American culture.

A single quote from Sun Zi reveals so many Chinese realities that are often unknown or ignored. Trying to understand Chinese culture by learning the language and its history can be long and difficult for foreigners. It requires an important personal investment which, for many, seems an impossible mission. In addition, the mainstream Western media tend to publish Chinese news without taking into account its cultural aspects, simply interpreting China according to Western standards and perceptions inherited from their own cultures. China and the United States are often referred to as two world powers but a country with a 5,000-year history does not interact with the world in the same way as a young country like the United States does. The U.S. became a sovereign country in 1776, a worldwide leader in all economic fields from the 1890s onwards, a mere 130 years ago.

Forty years of China's economic development have distressed the world. This trend will increase and accelerate in the years to come. Dr. Martin Jacques is a former Senior Fellow at the University of Cambridge and the London School of Economics and was for many years a journalist and editor for several mainstream Western media, including *The Sunday Times*, *The Times*, *The Observer* and *The Guardian*. He argues in his book *When China Rules the World* that China's rise to power will be distinct and that the West should not treat China as a traditional Western country. In a recent interview, Dr. Jacques predicted that by 2030, China will contribute 34% of the world's gross domestic product (GDP), the United States 15% and the European Union 13% (7).

In the coming years, China is likely to have a greater influence on daily life in the world and in the West. Its impact on the global economy will continue to shake things up. Understanding China as an economic partner for today and tomorrow is essential. This comprehension can only be gained through being fully aware of the importance of the cultural differences between China and the West. Like any other culture, the Chinese culture has its richness and constraints.

This practical guide invites its readers to perceive China from a cultural point of view. The main topics covered are: China today, cross-cultural management in business implementation, Chinese business etiquette, and the impact of Confucianism. It provides information, analysis and recommendations in the hope that it will contribute to a better understanding between the West and the East, the West and China.

China today

Cultural diversity

Putting China and Europe (including the region of Eastern Russia) in perspective, we see that the two regions share many essential commonalities: cultural diversity, historical richness, timing of the appearance of the founding philosophers, and territorial size. Like Europe, China is vast, old and populated. Yet the majority of Europeans have an outdated and inaccurate view about China. To them, China appears complex and mysterious. This unknown, faraway giant often arouses distrust and fear.

China has a population of 1.4 billion people living in an area of 9.6 million square kilometers. It is divided into twenty-three provinces (including the disputed province of Taiwan), four municipalities (Beijing, Shanghai, Tianjin, Chongqing), five autonomous regions (Inner Mongolia, Xinjiang, Ningxia, Tibet, Guangxi) and two special administrative regions (Hong Kong, Macao).

China's provinces, with important decision-making powers, are the highest administrative divisions. The four municipalities, directly subordinate to the central authority in Beijing, are positioned at the same level as the provinces and autonomous regions. They consist of an urban center surrounded by a much larger suburban area and a surrounding rural area. The autonomous regions are predominantly populated by ethnic minority groups, and each autonomous region has its own local government. Leaders of the autonomous regions are traditionally appointed by their ethnic groups. Hong Kong and Macao are designated as Special Administrative Regions (SARs) with an independent political and economic system.

The mainland extends from west to east for about 5,000 km and from north to south for about 4,000 km. Its coastal territory extends over 14,500 km. It shares its international borders with 14 countries, extending over 22,100 km.

China's cultural diversity is unique in the world. Fifty-six ethnic groups have lived together for thousands of years. There are about 360 styles of traditional opera, 60 types of traditional cuisine and more than 300 living languages and dialects. Mandarin is spoken by about 92% of Chinese who are of Han ethnicity. Since the founding of the PRC, the population of ethnic minority groups has been steadily increasing. The most recent population census, conducted by the Chinese government in 2010, puts Mongolians at about six million, Tibetans 6.2 million, Uighurs 10 million, Manchus 10.3 million, Huis 10.5 million and Zhuang 17 million. The first official Chinese census dates back to 1953 and put Mongolians at about 1.45 million, Tibetans 2.75 million, Uyghurs 3.61 million, Manchus 2.39 million, Huis 3.53 million and Zhuang 6.86 million. (8) The result of China's 2020 Census was announced on May 11, 2021. Compared with 2010, the Han population has been increased by 4.93% and the population of various ethnic minorities increased by 10.26%.

According to archaeological research, the history of Chinese civilization began at least 5,000 years ago. In the Chinese classic mythology text *Shan Hai Jing*, meaning "the story of the mountains and the ocean", descriptions and characters of ancient China regularly coincide with archaeological discoveries. Its author unknown, the Chinese consider it as a reference book describing the life of their ancestors more than 5,000 years ago.

Chinese historical records have listed 22 dynasties ruled by more than 500 emperors and spanning 4,100 years. Thanks to its unique traditional lunar calendar system, *Nónglì*, China is the only country that has been able to record its historical events year by year, without interruption, for four millennia. The Chinese are proud of their history and venerate their ancestors. Children and adults read the same historical and literary classics, recite the same poems and proverbs, and sing the same songs.

Internationally, China impresses above all by the immensity of its population and its gigantic market. Few people really know its social, political and economic system. Since 1978, China has implemented profound reforms in all its systems. At present, it has a socialist social system, a market economy with state intervention and a political system based on meritocracy and internal competition. These three systems operate in a society deeply influenced by the culture of Confucianism.

Social System

The Chinese education system is similarly organized to that of many countries in Europe: pre-school, primary, secondary, specialized, vocational, higher and university. All Chinese citizens must undergo nine years of compulsory education. There is currently a significant disparity between urban and rural, east and west, coastal and inland areas. In order to reduce and eliminate this disparity, the Chinese government has been investing huge resources for many years.

China has the world's largest education system, with nearly 370 million students and more than 15.5 million teachers in about 527,000 schools (Ministry of Education China, 2019) (9). This figure does not include higher and university education.

In the current education system, Chinese students generally enroll in kindergarten at the age of two or three and leave it at the age of six. Pre-school education is not compulsory. Many kindergartens are private. However, the government has played a more proactive role in promoting access to preschool education. It has made a national commitment to gradually universalize one to three years of pre-school education by 2020.

Higher education (including university education) has undergone enormous expansion in the first decade of the 21st century, entering a new phase that will allow more than half of the university-age population to have access to higher education. The gross enrollment rate in higher education rose from 21% in 2006 (10) to 48.1% in 2018 (11) throughout China. According to a statistical report on education published by the Chinese Ministry of Education in 2018, a total of 38.33 million students were enrolled in the country's higher education institutions. In June 2019, 8.34 million university graduates entered the labor market (12). China's 2020 census results show that, from 2010 to 2020, the number of people with a university education jumped by 73%, from 8,930 out of every 100,000 people to 15,467, and more than 218 million people now have a university education. During this period, an impressive number of institutions and programs were created. Mobility and international cooperation have been actively promoted. As a result, China's higher education system has become more efficient and diversified.

China's education system is huge, diverse and dynamic. It is managed by the state but is increasingly decentralized. In recent years, the Ministry of Education has moved from direct control to macro-level monitoring of the education system. It steers reform through laws, plans, budget allocation, information services, policy guidelines and administrative resources. The county level government has primary responsibility for the governance and delivery of school education. Provincial authorities administer institutions of higher education.

Vocational education has also made remarkable progress, the country has educated 270 million high-level and skilled workers in 70 years. (13)

China's education system has undergone continuous reforms since the early 1980s. From expanding access to promoting quality education as a core value, the government has been adjusting and steadily advancing education to make it compatible with social and economic development, as well as new educational needs and trends. The Chinese government prioritizes financial investment policy for public schools and legislative policy to stimulate and promote the establishment of private schools.

China's social system has been greatly inspired by those of various European countries, especially France and Germany. The Chinese characteristic is taken into account. The Chinese Social Insurance Law, which came into force on July 1, 2011, is based on five mandatory pillars: retirement insurance, health insurance, maternity insurance, unemployment insurance and occupational accident insurance (14). The objective was to set up the first social insurance system in the country.

In managing a huge population, China has established the youngest retirement age in the world, between 55 and 60 for men and between 50 and 55 for women. One of the reasons for this choice is to make it easier for the younger generations to take up employment.

Following recent improvements in the living standard, Chinese life expectancy has risen sharply. China today has about 250 million retired senior citizens (15), a figure expected to double in 20 years. This represents an enormous challenge for pension benefit management.

Since October 15, 2011, all foreign employees working in China are required to join the national social insurance system. The compulsory affiliation for foreign employees concerns all pillars of social security, in accordance with the provisions of the Social Insurance Law. Foreign employees have access to the five branches of social security on the same basis as Chinese nationals.

Political system

The Chinese political system (16) is constantly questioned and contested in the Western world which does not share the Chinese ruling party's ideology. However, this ideology of a social vision with authoritarian power is not only the outcome of the communist system but also the essence of 2,500 years of Confucianism. The country has always been ruled by a single authority and controlled by a community around an authoritarian power represented by an emperor.

China has been led by the Communist Party since 1949. State power is exercised through the National People's Congress, the judiciary and the State Council. Today, China's supreme political power is headed by the Politburo, which is managed by a seven-member committee chaired by Xi Jinping.

The National People's Congress is China's parliament and institution of legislative power. It meets once a year for a ten-day session in the Great Hall of the People in Beijing. Its 3,000 representatives are elected for five years through a voting system. It functions like a senate: its members are drawn from the executive bodies of the territories and are elected in each of the provinces or special regions. Its members are chosen through local elections and often come from the lowest ranks.

China's judicial system is one of the three branches of government, along with the executive and legislative branches. The Chinese constitution provides that judicial institutions are separate from the executive branch and must operate independently. However, it should be noted that the Chinese judiciary is currently an integral part of the administration and is under the leadership of the Communist Party.

People's courts are organized into three levels corresponding to administrative districts. Judges are appointed by the local assemblies at each level: district (or basic) people's courts, intermediate people's courts, and higher people's courts. Each level corresponds to a level of People's Procuratorate: Basic, Intermediate and Higher. According to the principle of two-tier jurisdiction, the decision of the second instance is final and each court may have jurisdiction in the first or second instance, depending on the seriousness of the case and according to legal provisions. The intermediate and higher courts, as well as the Supreme People's Court, are the appellate courts of the lower court that ruled in the first instance. The Supreme People's Court, with its seat in Beijing, is the court of first and last instance and China's highest judicial authority, with the exception of the SARs of Hong Kong and Macao which have independent judicial organizations. In addition, there are several special people's courts, such as military courts and maritime courts.

In 1980, 2004 and 2008, China initiated major reforms in its judicial system. The latest, in 2008, started from the people's demand to adopt the defense of their common interests as a fundamental task, with the promotion of social harmony as a guiding thread. The current task of this judicial reform has essentially been completed and concretized by the revision and improvement of the laws. Due to the continuous progress and development of China's economy and society, the national judicial reform is constantly continuing and deepening.

The State Council, corresponding to the central government, is the main administrative and executive authority of the PRC. It is chaired by the Prime Minister and comprises the government ministries and offices. There are approximately 50 members on the State Council. From 2018, the State Council of State Affairs is composed of the General Directorate, 29 ministries, commissions and administrations, 17 directly subordinate bodies, eight functional offices and a number of institutions. The Council meets once a month, while its Standing Committee meets twice a week. The members of the Standing Committee of the Council for State Affairs include the Prime Minister, the four Vice Prime Ministers, five Councilors for State Affairs, and the Secretary General.

Meritocracy system and kējǔ

The meritocratic selection system for civil servants has existed in China for 1,400 years. Chinese meritocracy is a concept based on an individual's knowledge, skills, virtues and intelligence. It emphasizes the link between an individual's merit and their access to power. The origin of the kējǔ system can be traced back to the year 605 when the emperor Sui Yang Di sought to recruit talent to help him realize ambitious projects. He invented this imperial examination system to identify the best candidates for civil servants.

In the ancient kējǔ system, the participants were tested on their abilities in school arts, military arts, civil law, income and taxes, agriculture and geography, and the Confucian Classics. The school arts included music, arithmetic, writing, and knowledge of rituals and ceremonies in public and private life. Military arts included military strategy, archery and chariot driving. Depending on historical periods or emperors' preferences, one or more of these subjects were more favored than others.

In ancient China, *kējǔ* offered people from underprivileged backgrounds an extraordinary opportunity for social ascension. The system operated on equal opportunity, equal treatment and equal rewards. All adult males from all walks of life could participate in the examination. Regardless of the participant's social background, the exam taken was the same. To avoid preferential treatment, participants' responses were copied by intermediaries and then scored by pre-assigned judges. In this way, handwriting recognition was not possible. The final winners were received by the emperor and rewarded according to the announced rules. For many, it was a chance to change their destiny.

The ancient *kējǔ* system was highly demanding. It consisted of three levels of tests, the local examination, the examination in the capital, and the examination of the finalists by the emperor himself. The failure rate could reach as high as 99%. The candidate's journey was long and difficult.

Kējǔ is recognized by Western experts as the fifth great Chinese invention. It was considered to be the fairest system of the time. Known in Europe as early as the 16th century, this Chinese imperial examination attracted great attention from contemporary European thinkers in the 17th century. Personalities such as the French philosopher Voltaire claimed that the Chinese had "perfected moral science" with *kējǔ*.

Kējǔ has inspired today's global examination system. It has evolved in China and continues today in the form of *Gāokǎo*, the annual university entrance examination.

Kējǔ was abolished in 1905, following the change of the Chinese regime. However, this meritocratic approach to choosing civil servants is rooted in Chinese culture and permeates the Chinese political system. Through numerous local and centralized examinations, civil servants are selected or promoted according to their knowledge, skills, experience and human qualities. To be appointed, a candidate must be the best at what they do and be appreciated by colleagues and superiors. Loyalty to the party, the country and the people is an important selection criterion. In addition, the candidate must have a thorough understanding of governance, possess the perspectives and competences as a team leader, adopt a democratic style of decision-making, and comply with regulations and laws.

The example of the political ascension of Chinese President Xi Jinping demonstrates how this practice works. Xi's father was a senior official in Mao's government. His family did not escape the sociopolitical purge during the Cultural

Revolution. At the age of 15, Xi was sent to a mountain region for re-education. For five years he worked in the fields, raising pigs and cleaning toilets, and lived in an earthen "cave house". During his professional career, he was elected mayor of his village, then promoted to be responsible for a county, a city and a province. After assuming various roles in local government and having travelled across more than half of China, Xi was elected Secretary General of the Communist Party of Shanghai in 2007. This allowed him to join the party's central committee in Beijing. He became China's president in 2012 after 40 years in politics.

A career as a civil servant such as Xi Jinping's is very common in China. Most senior Chinese politicians have a 30 to 40-year political career behind them, proving themselves by traveling the country and holding various positions. The rise of a civil servant in China is so difficult and perilous that the people describe it as "going to hell and back five times".

To finish the illustration of the Chinese political system, it is important to know a reality often unknown to outsiders. China is ruled by a single party, the Communist Party, but it is no secret to the Chinese people that internal competition within the party is fierce. The different tendencies form groups that are noticed, followed and commented on by the people. For example, the group with a patriotism tendency is called *Ying*, meaning "eagle", and is more nationalist and firmer in its foreign policy strategy. The group inspired by Confucianism is called *Ru* and is considered more moderate in its management of internal and external affairs. Finally, the pro-Western group is called *Xi*, meaning "the West". The complexity of China's political system is often labeled by Western scholars and experts as "totalitarian communism". This deserves more reflection and analysis.

Economic Development

The growth of the Chinese economy has broken all world records since its reforms. The Chinese government isn't able to get everything right in its economic development but, like any other government, it needs the recognition and support of its own people in the implementation of its economic strategy in order to ensure its sustainability and legitimacy. Forty years ago, China was emerging from several years of deadly famine. It then went from a country of extreme poverty to a nation of great economic power, becoming the largest in terms of purchasing power parity in 2014 and second-largest in terms of nominal GDP in 2015. In 40 years, China has gradually reformed its economic system which moved from a closed, agriculture-based economy to a market-oriented economy.

Its economic system has a strongly mixed character, composed of state-owned, collective and private enterprises. Collective enterprises are those with a mixed participation of local governments and private companies. Private enterprises are strongly represented by family businesses and complemented by joint ventures and Wholly Foreign-Owned Enterprises (WFOEs). Joint ventures are owned by Chinese and foreign investors; WFOEs are entirely owned by foreign investors.

State-owned enterprises (SOEs) continue to be the backbone of national economic development. In 2018, the number of employees working in SOEs represented 15.7% of the total while the number of SOEs represented only 1.3% of the total (17). In the latest *Fortune* Global 500 ranking, China for the first time has more companies than the United States. The ranking is based on the 2019 turnover, with a breakdown of 124 Chinese and 121 American companies on the list. Ninety-one percent of the 124 Chinese companies are state-owned.

Nevertheless, according to a report of the National Bureau of Statistics of China, the number of private companies represented 84.1% of all Chinese companies in 2018 (18). The constantly growing Chinese private sector contributes to more than 60% of national GDP growth and generates more than half of China's tax revenues (19).

In the 1970s, 100% of Chinese companies were state-owned. After the 1978 reforms, China greatly reduced state intervention and adopted measures to increase the role of private capital. It offers more and more possibilities for combining public and private capital. This signals the end of state monopolies in various sectors such as railways, air transport, finance, energy and telecoms. There are also opportunities to create private banks. A crucial change occurred when the entry of foreign capital into China was allowed in the 1980s and when the stock exchanges were reopened in 1990.

Adopting a market economy with state intervention, China has achieved tremendous growth in many strategic areas after four decades of development.

International Trade

China has been a member of the World Trade Organization (WTO) since December 2001. For 20 years, it has recorded consistent trade surpluses. According to 2019 figures, it had a trade surplus of about USD 430 billion by engaging in USD 4,568 billion of global trade. As the world's largest exporter and importer, it exported USD 2,499 billion and imported USD 2,069 billion worth of goods worldwide. (20) (21)

China's top 10 export products in 2019 were electrical equipment and machinery, furniture, lighting, signs, prefabricated buildings, plastic goods, vehicles, optical, technical and medical devices, clothing and accessories, iron and steel goods, toys and games. They accounted for about two-thirds (67.6%) of the total value of its global shipments. (22)

China's top 10 import products were electrical equipment and machinery, electronic equipment and machinery, mineral fuels including petroleum, ores, slag and ash, plastic goods, vehicles, optical, technical and medical devices, gems, precious metals, organic chemicals and copper. They accounted for approximately 77.3% of the total value of its global imports. (23)

In 2019, China exported to more than 120 countries and imported from about 80 countries. About 49% of its exports were to Asian countries, 20% to the United States and 20% to Europe. It exported mainly to the following countries or regions: United States (USD 418.6 billion), Hong Kong (USD 279.6 billion), Japan (USD 143.2 billion), South Korea (USD 111 billion), Vietnam (USD 98 billion) and Germany (USD 79.7 billion). (24)

Around 55.4% of Chinese imports were purchased from Asian countries, 18.1% from European countries and 8% from North American suppliers. China's imports were mainly from South Korea (USD 203 billion), Japan (USD 180 billion), Taiwan (USD 177 billion), the United States (USD 156 billion) and Germany (USD 106 billion). (24)

In October 2020, China reported strong growth in international trade for the month of September. Exports and imports in USD increased by 9.9% and 13.2%, respectively, compared to the previous year. Despite the ongoing trade war and strained relations between the U.S. and China, Chinese export growth to the U.S. rose to 20.4% year-on-year in September with the highest value since June 2012. WTO data showed that China's international trade accounted for 12.6% of the world total, up 1% from the same period a year earlier. (25)

On November 15, 2020, China signed the RCEP (Regional Comprehensive Economic Partnership) agreement with fourteen Asian countries to launch the largest free trade zone in the world. RCEP represents about 30% of the world population, world GDP and world trade. "The signing of RCEP is not only a historic achievement of regional cooperation in East Asia, but also a victory for multilateralism and free trade in the world," China's Prime Minister Li Keqiang said at the signing ceremony. (26)

Technology

The development and transfer of technology have always been important for many industries in the Chinese economy since the early days of the open market policy. In 1990, no one in China was yet familiar with the Internet. Today, China has the largest number of Internet users in the world.

The high-tech industry, with high growth and high value-added characteristics, is a strategic leading industry in China's national economy and plays a key role in industrial restructuring and the transformation of its economic development model.

1. 5G Technology

There is a global consensus that the country leading the deployment of 5G (fifth generation) technology could gain an advantage in the development of future technologies. China has become a leader in the development of 5G wireless mobile networks.

Forty years ago, Shenzhen, a Chinese city bordering Hong Kong, was a poor fishing village of 20,000 inhabitants. In August 2020, this city of 13 million inhabitants became the first in the country to achieve full 5G coverage, with 46,000 5G base stations installed. In September 2020, China celebrated the 40th anniversary of Shenzhen as its first Special Economic Zone.

In the first quarter of 2020, Chinese companies ranked number 1 worldwide with a 75% share of the global 5G network devices market (27). By the end of July 2020, 5G users in China had surpassed 88 million, representing 80% of global users (28). The initial target for the number of 5G base stations to be installed was 600,000 by 2020, but the Chinese government confirmed that 700,000 stations had already been installed in mid-November 2020 (29).

The 5G service is active in a number of sectors in China, including manufacturing, health, media and transportation. During the Covid-19 pandemic, Chinese companies actively explored the benefits of 5G technology to introduce applications to the areas such as healthcare, education and teleworking.

The world had barely begun to use 5G when China already embarked on 6G. China's Ministry of Science and Technology announced on November 6, 2019 that it had formed two teams to oversee 6G research and study. This marked the official start of a state-sponsored effort to accelerate the development of this technology. One team, consisting of government departments, would be responsible for advancing the implementation of 6G technology, while the other, consisting of 37 experts from universities, scientific institutions and companies, would provide technical advice for major government decisions. China successfully put the first 6G communication test satellite into orbit on November 6, 2020, from its satellite launch center in Taiyuan, Shanxi Province, in northern China.

While 5G is known to have data transmission speeds at least 10 times faster than 4G (deployed in 2009), it is too early to tell what 6G might be or what types of technologies it would advance. However, Huawei already announced in April 2021 its intention to launch 6G technology by 2030.

2. Artificial Intelligence (AI)

China's interest in AI is relatively recent—it started working in this field in 2011—so its researchers are generally less experienced than Americans. Only 25% of Chinese AI workers have more than 10 years' experience compared to 50% of American workers (30). Nevertheless, China has some advantages in this field.

With a population of 1.4 billion people, China has a huge reservoir of data to advance its research. The world's leading research centers, such as Tsinghua University, Shanghai Jiaotong University and the Chinese Academy of Sciences, provide brilliant brainpower to make significant breakthroughs in research and development.

A growing number of educated people also allows China to find talent within its borders. China is tirelessly working on initiatives to increase AI-related education at the university level. In 2018, the Ministry of Education announced a plan to promote AI education. Several major universities had already added AI departments and majors to their programs.

To promote the development of AI, the Chinese government has launched a series of AI industrial parks in the east and south of the country. By 2018, China had more than 60 AI technology parks. Industrial parks generally have preferential policies, such as rental subsidies and tax incentives, to attract companies. (30)

The applications of AI in various Chinese industries are remarkable. These industries include manufacturing, advertising, new retail, food and beverage, hospitality, gaming, healthcare, and transportation. The current applications of AI technology in the healthcare sector are impressive. They include medical imaging, diagnostics, drug discovery, health management and disease prevention.

During the Covid-19 outbreak, China experienced unprecedented advances in AI technology. According to a WHO report, China used its advanced AI technology during the outbreak with great efficiency. Some of these technologies were used to control the epidemic, such as surveillance, fever detection and QR codes, while others were used in diagnosis, such as smart scanners. AI technology was also exploited for public health purposes, with disinfectant robots and real-time maps showing the location of active infections.

In the field of transportation, robotaxis are the first market for autonomous cars. A number of robotaxi projects have been launched in the last two years in China. Chinese companies such as Baidu, AutoX (backed by Alibaba) and DiDi (the king of ride-sharing services) have launched projects in Guangzhou and Shanghai, with Chinese consumers queuing up to take a ride in self-service cabs. According to market research firm McKinsey & Company, China has the potential to become the world's largest market for autonomous vehicles, potentially accounting for up to 66% of passenger-kilometers travelled by 2040. This would generate USD 1,100 billion in revenue from mobility services and USD 900 billion from sales of autonomous vehicles. In unit terms, this means that autonomous vehicles would account for over 40% of new vehicle sales and 12% of the installed base of vehicles in 2040. (31)

The size of the Chinese AI market is growing at a dizzying rate. It reached 33.9 billion renminbi (RMB) in 2018 and the compound annual growth rate was more than 44% between 2015 and 2018. By the end of 2020, the market size was expected to reach RMB 71 billion. (30)

In 2018, the value of investment in China's AI industry reached RMB 131.1 billion, an increase of about RMB 67.7 billion from 2017 (30). Today, the scale of investment puts China at the top of the world rankings. Although the growth of AI financing events slowed in 2018, the total value of investment has increased significantly. Major financing events frequently occurred and allocated capital was more concentrated for the moment in large companies.

China's AI industry is becoming one of its most important markets and could become one of the largest in the world. However, its AI market is not yet mature and there is still plenty of room for development. China wants to become the world's largest hub for AI innovation by 2030. To begin with, it hosted for the first time in Shanghai the World Artificial Intelligence Conference in 2019 to promote AI innovation worldwide. More than 150 leading figures from the global AI industry and academic circles attended the conference, as well as 300 domestic and foreign companies. (32)

3. Space industry

China's space program accompanied the country's rapid economic growth during the 1990s, with programs covering the entire spectrum of space activity: telecommunications, Earth observation, meteorological, navigation and military reconnaissance satellites. Its ambitious short-term development plan included the realization of a space station in low orbit, the sending of robots to the surface of the Moon, and the development of launchers.

China currently has a complete family of Long March launchers. The first flight of its Long March 5 heavy launcher took place on November 3, 2016, enabling China to develop a new family of advanced launchers.

On January 3, 2019, during the Chang'e 4 mission, China sent a module to the dark side of the Moon, never before explored by humans. This has paved the way for even more ambitious projects, such as the construction of a Chinese space station, the exploration of Mars, and manned space flights. The manned space program has already been launched, resulting in a first manned flight in 2003 and the launch of the Tiangong 1 prototype space station in 2011.

The launch of the Long March 5 rocket on December 27, 2019 crowned a momentous year for China's space program. After several failures, the spacecraft succeeded in carrying a China-made satellite into orbit. This launcher, the most powerful in the national arsenal, with a capacity of 25 tons, has allowed China to see further and bigger. With this launch, China became the country that carried out the most launches in 2019 (34, including 32 successful), ahead of the United States (27). In all, China carried out 39 launches in 2020 and plans to carry out more than 40 launches in 2021.

It succeeded on June 22, 2020 in launching its latest BeiDou Navigation Satellite System (BDS) which offers an alternative to America's GPS or Europe's Galileo. It consists of about thirty satellites that cover the entire Earth.

Launched on November 24, 2020, China's Chang'e 5 mission was successfully completed on December 16, 2020. Nearly two kg of lunar samples were brought back to Earth in the first mission of its kind since that led by the former USSR in 1976. This ambitious operation allowed China to test new technologies, crucial to its goal of sending astronauts to the Moon by 2030.

China's goal is clear: to become the world's leading space power by 2030. It wanted to launch its first Martian probe, deploy a new lunar probe and send into space the central core of its future inhabited space station. On April 29, 2021, China launched into orbit its Tianhe core module, the first of three components of China's space station. In orbit around the planet Mars, the Chinese spacecraft Tianwen-1, dropped a lander on May 15, 2021 that contained Zhurong, a rover named after a Chinese mythological god of fire. The most perilous stage of the ten-month mission has thus been completed. An interesting fact is that China started its research on the Mars mission only in 2016, whereas the United States and Russia began investing in it 50 years ago. The Organization for Economic Cooperation and Development estimated the Chinese space budget at more than USD 8.4 billion in 2017 (33), still far behind the USD 48 billion in civilian and military spending by the United States (33), according to analyst Phil Smith of BryceTech.

Infrastructure

When Chinese Premier Li Keqiang presented his government's annual work report in Beijing in May 2020, the new infrastructure initiative was at the top of the agenda. This initiative is expected to generate massive investment over the next five years.

1. High-speed railways

After unveiling the prototype of a high-speed train capable of reaching 600 km/h in 2019, the country betted on this driverless train. At the very end of 2019, China opened its first fully automated, 174 km-long, high-speed line between Beijing and

Zhangjiakou. The train reaches a maximum speed of 350 km/h, connecting the two cities in 47 minutes (for the fastest connections) instead of three hours. It will serve the Olympic sites for the Winter Olympics in 2022 (34).

According to data from China State Railway Group, the operational length of Chinese railways reached 141,400 kilometers at the end of July 2020, ranking second in the world. High-speed railways were 36,000 kilometers, making them the world's longest. (35)

In August 2020, China State Railway Group published an outline of its railway plan which defines the development goals and main tasks to be accomplished by 2035. This includes a national railway network of more than 200,000 kilometers, including about 70,000 kilometers of high-speed tracks, and an intelligent railway using 5G technology and the BDS. (36) Chinese railways will be extended to cities with 200,000 or more inhabitants, and high-speed rail will cover cities with more than 500,000 inhabitants. (37)

The 5G and BDS technologies will be used to form an integrated train control system using data collected both on the ground and in space. With the new technologies, the train control system will have more accurate positioning, guarantee enhanced safety, shorten the interval between trains, and improve transport capacity by more than 30%.

On the energy saving plan, if the new train control system is adopted, a Beijing-Shanghai round trip on the high-speed railway could save about 9,000 kilowatt hours of electricity.

2. Airports

In the span of a decade, China has gone from a country where few people had the opportunity to travel by air to a nation where millions of citizens fly not only within its vast territory but also to destinations around the world.

China currently has about 235 airports, but many do not have the capacity to support the coming increase in passengers and flights. Government officials estimate that about 450 airports will be needed across the country by 2035. (38) Already equipped with some of the world's largest airports, China is continuing its construction project, averaging 14 airports per year over the next 15 years.

Inaugurated in September 2019, the new Beijing Daxing International Airport is designed to handle more than 100 million passengers per year. It has four runways and a terminal the size of 97 soccer fields. For the first time, an airport is equipped with two departure floors and two arrival floors.

The airport also deploys new technologies, such as its baggage sorting system and facial recognition. New technologies have made it possible to reduce the walking distance in one of the world's largest terminals. Thanks to a unique layout and design, Daxing's passengers can easily reach their boarding gates.

The advantage of building new airports from scratch is that each facility can be developed to meet the demands of today's high technology, while keeping future growth in mind.

Today's airports are not stand-alone facilities. Daxing has a very efficient link with other modes of transportation such as major arterial roads and the high-speed rail network. Its terminal is directly linked to the multimodal transportation hub located underground. There is direct access from the terminal to the high-speed and metro lines. A new highway has already been completed to quickly connect the new airport to the city center at Beijing's 4th Ring Road level.

The Chinese don't consider this project to be excessive. There are three international airports in New York and five in London, while Beijing has only just opened its second. In the years to come, Shanghai, which has more than 24 million inhabitants, will build its third, and Guangzhou, with a population of 17 million, will build its second.

According to the International Air Transport Association (IATA), China's aviation industry is on its way to overtake the U.S. and will become the largest in the world by 2024. Between 2014 and 2019, China spent RMB 486.32 billion (USD 70 billion) on ground infrastructure, airport modernization and air traffic control systems. The Civil Aviation Administration of China budgeted RMB 85 billion (USD 12.2 billion) for aviation investment in fixed assets in 2019, and RMB 100 billion (USD 14.4 billion) in 2020. (39)

3. Chinese aircraft COMAC C919

International commercial aviation is currently managed by a duopoly. Aircraft manufacturers Boeing and Airbus account for an overwhelming majority of market share. They are both Western companies with headquarters in the United States (Boeing) and France (Airbus). But there is a new competitor on the scene.

Aircraft manufacturing is part of China's long-term goal to become the leader in technology and heavy manufacturing. By developing its own aircraft industry, an area where the country currently remains dependent on Western suppliers, China will keep billions of dollars at home and have its own airliner, free of customs duties.

The C919 aircraft development program was launched in 2008 by the Commercial Aircraft Corporation of China (COMAC). At least 200 companies and 20 universities in 20 Chinese provinces are involved in this construction project, and at least 17 companies have been created for the needs of this project. These include a wiring company jointly owned by Shanghai Aircraft Manufacturing Company (51%) and the French company Safran Electrical & Power (49%). Safran is additionally involved in supplying the complete propulsion system for the aircraft, including the engine, nacelle and thrust reverser. (40)

Safran has been present in China for more than 100 years and has forged numerous partnerships with key players in the Chinese aviation industry. The group equips the engines and autopilots of more than half of the helicopters in service in the country. Forty percent of airliners in service in China use landing gear or brakes designed by Safran. The group currently has more than 1,800 employees in some 20 entities in China. (41)

The C919 aircraft made a successful maiden flight on May 5, 2017 and entered a new phase of intensive test flights in the second half of 2020. COMAC announced that it had received 815 aircraft orders from 28 Chinese and foreign customers. It is expected to obtain its airworthiness certificate from the country's civil aviation authorities in 2021.

China is committed to developing two models of airliners and two models of regional aircraft, the C919 and CR929 narrow-body airliners, respectively, as well as the ARJ21 regional jets and MA60 series turboprops.

IATA has predicted that China is expected to become the world's largest market by mid-2020. IATA in November 2020 revised its performance outlook for the global airline industry in 2020 and 2021. Although important industry losses have incurred in 2020 and will continue in 2021, overall performance is expected to improve over the next year. Ever determined and patient, China is leading the recovery of the world's airline industry with large domestic demand that will allow carriers to register profits. Even if it takes a whole generation, thanks to its aircraft manufacturing capabilities, China is heading towards a great aeronautical future.

4. Bridges

Driven by the enormous demand for construction since China's economic reform and opening, the construction of bridges has surged both quantitatively and qualitatively. It has evolved in three major stages, from follower to competitor to leader. China has built 90 of the 100 tallest bridges of this century, including the highest bridge and longest sea bridge in the world.

In December 2016, the Beipanjiang Bridge, 565 meters above the void, was inaugurated in one of the most mountainous regions of the country, in southwest China. Connecting the provinces of Guizhou and Yunnan, this 1,341-meter-long suspension bridge won the title of highest bridge in the world from its compatriot Sidu River Bridge in Hubei Province in central China.

Numbers alone mean little if we ignore the influence of these structures. By dividing travel time by four, Beipanjiang Bridge benefits a regional population of 81 million. Moreover, by constituting a section linked with the G56 highway, the bridge connects the city of Hangzhou to the city of Ruili (on the border with Burma and bordering Tibet), by a 2,900-kilometer-long highway.

Innovation is another important factor in China's bridge achievements. The Hong Kong-Zhuhai-Macao Bridge is a series of bridges and tunnels linking Zhuhai (Guangdong Province), Hong Kong and Macao across the Pearl River Delta in southern China.

The infrastructure between Lantau Island in Hong Kong and the artificial island of Zhuhai-Macao consists of two times three lanes of traffic roads, four tunnels and four artificial islands. The main bridge is built to accommodate 40,000 vehicles every day, including shuttle buses that run every ten minutes. It was designed to last 120 years. Its steel superstructure weighs 420,000 tons (60 times the mass of the Eiffel Tower) and can withstand natural phenomena (typhoon level 16 and earthquake level 8). This 22.8-kilometer-long main bridge crosses the waters of Zhuhai through three suspension bridges with piers ranging from 280 to 460 meters, and viaducts with piers ranging from 75 to 110 meters. The support pylons adopt different shapes: Chinese knot, dolphin and sail.

An underwater tunnel passage leads to the outskirts of Lantau Island. Two artificial islands join the eastern and western ends of the 6.7-kilometer-long tunnel. The submarine section leaves the major maritime corridors of the Pearl River estuary and the air corridors of the Hong Kong International

Airport free of infrastructure. The route then runs along Lantau Island for 12 kilometers.

Construction began on December 15, 2009, its official inauguration took place on October 23, 2018, and its opening to the public on October 24, 2018. It is the longest maritime bridge in the world. In January 2018, the estimated construction cost of the 55-kilometer-long project was RMB 120 billion (USD 18.4 billion).

In China, about 67% of the country's land is made up of mountains, hills and plateaus. Forty percent of China's territory lies above 2,000 meters. There are many high-altitude mountains, especially in the southwest, which almost entirely comprises mountains. China has more than 1,500 rivers, with a basin area of more than 1,000 square kilometers.

China's development efforts must extend to all mountains and rivers. From 2016 to 2020, China's transport investment was expected to exceed RMB 16 trillion (USD 2,390 billion), with a substantial share reserved for bridge construction. (42)

E-commerce

The Internet arrived in China in 1994. Over the past 20 years, it has penetrated all industrial and commercial sectors of the country. The fundamental changes brought about by the Internet have been integrated into the operations of traditional industrial markets. The e-commerce industry has developed and affected the Chinese economy with surprising speed.

The e-commerce sector has demonstrated an explosive growth dynamic. Innovations brought by the application of technologies to e-commerce have stimulated entrepreneurship. Chinese SMEs are the biggest beneficiaries. Thanks to e-commerce platforms, they can compete with large companies on an equal footing and they can benefit from affordable digital services, which were previously too expensive. China's small entrepreneurs use these platforms to build brand awareness, acquire and manage customers, and drive innovation.

The growth rates of the e-commerce market are very high and China has become not only one of the most important markets but also one of the most fascinating. Cross-border e-commerce is opening up with China's strategy of "Bring In" and "Go Global" policies. It has become a new engine of China's rapid economic development that also offers huge opportunities for small foreign companies. But the biggest challenge for them is how to enter and successfully stay on these Chinese platforms. Today, almost all major foreign brands have one or more virtual stores on these platforms. This is unavoidable and becomes almost mandatory.

E-commerce is particularly well developed in the country's first-ranked cities known as Tier-1 cities: Shanghai, Beijing, Guangzhou and Shenzhen. The gap between Tier 1 and Tiers 2, 3 and 4 is gradually narrowing, thanks to the rapid development of the whole country. However, there is still great potential for development in Chinese e-commerce.

For the time being, the major suppliers of these Chinese e-commerce platforms are few. Alibaba Group, the largest company in China's e-commerce sector, provides infrastructure and online market places for B2B, B2C and C2C businesses. Its market valuation reached RMB 4,100 billion (USD 585.1 billion) as of June 30, 2020. For 2019, the domestic retail sales of the three Chinese e-commerce giants Alibaba, JD and Pinduoduo reached RMB 6,600 billion, RMB 2,000 billion and RMB 1,000 billion, respectively. The total sales of these three platforms account for 90% of China's online retail sales and 22% of total retail sales. (43)

Today, millions of Chinese consumers connect daily to the Internet and buy a very wide range of products. Almost everything can be found on Chinese e-commerce platforms. The size and growth rate of the e-commerce market in China is unique. With more than 940 million Internet users at the end of June 2020 (44), China had more online users than the United States. The number of e-commerce users in China is expected to reach 1,093 million in 2024. (45).

Chinese e-commerce players are less experienced, less mature but more innovative than their American counterparts. China has the potential to become the world's largest market for almost everything and e-commerce should be no exception.

Renewable Energy

China is the world's leading producer of electricity from renewable energy sources. Its renewable energy sector is growing faster than its fossil fuel and nuclear capacity. It currently has the world's largest installed hydro, solar and wind power capacity. The country sees renewable energy as a source of energy security and carbon emission reduction.

According to data published by the China Renewable Energy Engineering Institute, the total installed capacity of renewable energy in China by the end of 2018 was 1,900 GW, an increase of 6.7% compared to 2017. According to China's National Energy Administration, the country's renewable energy output reached 2,214.80 GW in 2020, an increase of 8.4% from 2019.

The website Statista.com is a German online portal offering statistics from institute data, market and opinion research as well as data from the economic sector. According to its report, Chinese investment in clean energy is the highest in the world. In 2019, China injected USD 83.4 billion into research and development, followed by the United States and Japan, with USD 55.5 billion and USD 16.5 billion, respectively. These three countries accounted for about 71% of total global investment.

Renewable energy systems can be built and used wherever there is enough water, wind and sun. One of China's major challenges is to bring energy from production sites to the place of consumption. For example, by 2017, more than 30% of the renewable energy produced in the sunny and windy provinces of Xinjiang and Gansu in northwest China had never been used because it could not be delivered where it was needed. The densely populated megacities in eastern China, such as Shanghai and Beijing, are thousands of kilometers away from the production sites in the northwest.

The Chinese government has invested billions of dollars in high-voltage power lines to transmit the energy produced in the sunny and windy regions of China's vast expanse. This includes a RMB 22.6 billion (USD 3.17 billion) investment line of 1,600 kilometers, started from Qinghai Province in western China. Completed in May 2020, the line crosses the Gansu River to reach Henan Province, in the center of the country. (46)

The benefits of developing the renewable energy industry are numerous. One is to enable job creation and support long-term economic growth. China has created more than four million jobs in recent years, accounting for 39% of total global employment in this sector (47) and became a world leader in renewable energy in 2019.

As China's renewable energy manufacturing has developed, the cost of renewable energy technologies has dropped significantly. Innovation has helped, but the main driver of cost reduction has been market expansion. Along with it, China has the political incentive, economic capacity and moral consensus to lead the global renewable energy sector. Following the Covid-19 epidemic and its severe social and economic impact, China has energetically stimulated its economic recovery. The provinces have announced their investment plans, in which new infrastructure plays an extremely important role. This infrastructure will also positively affect the development of China's energy sector in the post-epidemic era.

Digital currency

The EU has dangled the prospect of launching a digital euro and the U.S. Federal Reserve is exploring the digital dollar. China's central bank has made steady progress towards its goal of launching the world's first major sovereign digital currency. "China must become the first country to issue a digital currency in order to reduce its dependence on the global dollar payment system," the People's Bank of China said in a commentary published in its September 2020 magazine.

The Chinese government explained in mid-2020 that the country's four major state-owned banks had begun large-scale internal testing of the digital portfolio in RMB. China Construction Bank, Bank of China, Industrial and Commercial Bank of China and Agricultural Bank of China are currently testing the digital RMB with the central bank in major cities.

China Central Television (CCTV) reported in August 2020 that in Suzhou, a city near Shanghai, some government officials had received part of their salary in digital RMB.

In mid-October 2020, China publicly tested the digital RMB in Shenzhen, Guangdong Province (southern China). The local government and the Chinese central bank together donated 50,000 digital red packets each containing RMB 200. This was the first time that the digital currency test was made public after a series of internal tests.

In December 5, 2020, in a second public test of its digital currency, Suzhou issued 100,000 red packets of digital RMB worth a total of RMB 20 million (USD 3.06 million), each containing RMB 200, to local residents. Analysts noted that this new series of tests involved a wider range of consumption and application scenarios compared to the first public trial.

These tests are expected to expand to more cities in the short term. The digital RMB will also be tested at the 2022 Winter Olympic Games in Beijing. For the world, the issuance and circulation of China's digital currency will certainly lead to massive changes in international finance.

BRI and AIIB

The Belt and Road Initiative (BRI), formerly known as One Belt One Road, or OBOR, is a global infrastructure development strategy proposed by the Chinese government in 2013. By the end of 2019, the initiative involved massive investments in nearly 167 countries and international organizations (48). The Chinese government describes the BRI as "an attempt to improve regional connectivity and embrace a better future". The project has a target completion time of 2049, which coincides with the 100th anniversary of the founding of the PRC.

Reminiscent of the ancient Chinese Silk Road, the BRI is a vast infrastructure project that would extend from East Asia to Europe. The BRI is a transcontinental program of long-term political and investment policy aimed at developing infrastructure and accelerating the economic integration of countries along the historic Silk Road.

The BRI combines two initiatives: (1) The Silk Road Land Economic Belt, comprising six development corridors; and (2) the 21st Century Maritime Silk Road. China's BRI, sometimes referred to as the New Silk Road, is one of the most ambitious infrastructure projects ever conceived.

The Asian Infrastructure Investment Bank (AIIB), first proposed in October 2013, is a development bank dedicated to lending for BRI infrastructure projects. In 2015, China announced that more than RMB 1 trillion (USD 160 billion) of infrastructure projects were being planned or built.

AIIB is a multilateral development bank that aims to improve economic and social performance in Asia. The bank currently has 103 members and 21 potential members from around the world. The bank began operations after the agreement came into force on December 25, 2015.

An administrative budget of USD 188 million and a capital budget of USD 6.7 million were approved to support the achievement of the institutional priorities and work of the AIIB, according to the programs outlined in the 2020 Business Plan. AIIB planned to commit approximately USD 4 to 5 billion on 20 to 30 projects in 2020.

***

In 2002, China had 80 million middle-class people. After 20 years of dazzling economic development, it now has a middle class of about 500 million people. This figure could reach 700 million in two years' time. However, nearly 600 million Chinese, or 40% of the population, still live in rural areas. The Chinese government's decades-long fight against poverty has had a significant impact on these regions.

China announced at the end of November 2020 that its last nine extremely poor counties, all located in the southwestern province of Guizhou, have eradicated absolute poverty (according to the standards of the United Nations). It means that all 832 counties registered in China have now been lifted out of extreme poverty. Nevertheless, to break poverty in the most isolated regions, China still has a long way to go. To bridge the gap between the relative wealth of its urban areas and the poverty of its countryside, China's economic development will continue and accelerate.

As China's development in trade expands, it will soon find itself in a position of decision-maker rather than follower, as it has been until now. It will influence the way of living and working in the world and in the West. It also means that there will be interesting business opportunities for Chinese and foreign companies in the decades to come. The importance of understanding China as an economic partner for today and tomorrow has become obvious more than ever.

Cross-cultural management
in business implementation

Faced with a modern and determined China enjoying constant and dynamic economic growth, foreign multinational companies have armed themselves with huge means to conquer this market of 1.4 billion consumers. According to a report published by the Ministry of Commerce of China at the Qingdao Multinationals Summit 2019, China has attracted more foreign investment than any other developing country for 27 consecutive years. The same report revealed that the creation of 961,000 foreign-owned enterprises had been recorded by the end of 2018, and that the actual use of this foreign capital had reached USD 2,100 billion. (49)

The most important American companies operate in China. Kentucky Fried Chicken (KFC) sells more chicken in China than in the United States. General Motors (GM) sells more than three million cars annually in the Chinese market (50). The number of Pizza Hut franchises in China more than quadrupled from 2009 to 2019 (51). Meanwhile, McDonald's Corp. opened its 2,000th store in China in 2014 and by the end of 2020 the number of stores had reached 3,790.

Apple doubled its market value in just over two years to become the first U.S. company to record a market capitalization of USD 1 trillion in August 2018 and, roughly two years later, became the first publicly traded U.S. company to surpass USD 2 trillion. Its success is closely related to its strategy in the Chinese market over the last decade. Apple has successfully integrated itself into the world's factory. China will soon be its largest consumer market, estimated at USD 44 billion. It is currently Apple's third-largest market, behind the United States and Europe. Apple achieves about 20% of its turnover on the Chinese market. The American technology giant reported a turnover of USD 9.33 billion in China for the company's third fiscal quarter ending June 2020, an increase of 1.9% compared to the same period for the previous year. The Chinese market is so important to Apple that it has decided to integrate China's BeiDou Navigation Satellite System into its iPhone models. Apart from Apple, other American companies, such as Tesla, Qualcomm and Boeing, have had enormous success in the Chinese market despite the ongoing trade war between the two countries.

Betting on China becoming the world's largest market for the Tesla Model 3, the American electric vehicle (EV) manufacturer in 2019 built a gigantic factory in Shanghai at a miraculous speed of just 10 months. Within a few months, the

Tesla Model 3 became the best-selling EV in China, with 45,800 units sold in the first half of 2020. In the quarter ending June 30, 2020, Tesla's revenues in China rose by 102.9% over the same period in 2019 to USD 1.4 billion, according to its financial results filed with the U.S. Securities and Exchange Commission. That meant China accounted for 23.3% of Tesla's total revenues of USD 6 billion in the quarter, compared to approximately 11% for the same period a year before.

European companies are also very active in China. According to the European Commission, the total value of trade between the European Union (EU) and China amounted to EUR 560 billion in 2019, making China the EU's second-largest economic partner after the United States, with trade of EUR 616 billion (52). In the first nine months of 2020, trade between the EU and China reached EUR 425.5 billion, compared to EUR 412.5 billion between the EU and the United States, according to the latest data published by Eurostat. China has thus become, for the first time, the EU's largest trading partner. (53)

Since the beginning of the Covid-19 epidemic, the number of rail freight transports between Europe and China has massively increased. Up to July 2020, more than 1,000 trains had been put into service for three consecutive months and double-digit growth had been recorded for five consecutive months. The China-Europe Express has become a microcosm of the increasingly close economic and commercial exchange between China and Europe in the post-epidemic era. (54)

In August 2020, the first direct train between Austria and China was inaugurated. With 41 containers of fiber products from the Austrian Lenzing Group, the train covered 10,460 kilometers in 16 days, starting its journey from Vienna station, passing through the Chinese city of Xian, and finally arriving in Shanghai. The connection of the Silk Road to the dense and efficient network of the Austrian Rail Cargo Group enabled the train to reach Chinese customers twice as fast.

According to China Railway Container Transport Corp. Ltd. data, China-Europe freight trains collectively ran 11,270 cargo trips between January and November 2020, an increase of 51% year-on-year. The round-trip rate reached 76% with a 98% heavy container rate. This includes 29 cities in China that have moved more than 100 trains to 90 cities in 20 European countries. (55)

On the one hand, in the context of the difficult recovery of international trade, European companies have continuously shipped local products to China to seize the opportunity of the first recovery of Chinese demand and the enormous potential of the Chinese market. On the other hand, European multinationals continue to invest and expand their activities in and cooperation with China.

In May 2020, Germany's Volkswagen Group announced an investment of EUR 2.1 billion in China to vigorously promote the development of its EV business and confirmed a further EUR 15 billion investment in September. In July, the French group Danone announced that it would invest EUR 100 million to support its R&D and innovation activities in China. In mid-August, KION Group AG, a German manufacturer well known for its forklift trucks and supply chain solutions, expanded its activities in China and laid the foundations for the construction of an additional counter-balanced truck production plant in the Chinese city of Jinan. The plant covers an area of 223,000 square meters and is scheduled to be operational in 2022.

A large number of non-Western multinationals also operate in China. For example, the Japanese car manufacturers Toyota, Mitsubishi and Subaru, as well as the giant Korean multinationals Samsung, Hyundai, Lucky Goldstar (LG) and Kia.

Despite the challenges presented by the Covid-19 pandemic, foreign companies continue to show their strong commitment to the Chinese market. Some of their local factories have posted record production figures and new investment projects have been launched.

Even with their strong interests and important investments, all Western companies agree on one point: getting to grips with the local culture is a major challenge in the Chinese market. There are many misunderstandings between the Chinese and Western parties. Frustrations from delays or failures are numerous. Despite the desire for cooperation on both sides, cultural differences impede it.

Western companies often mistakenly believe that if something works in the rest of the world, it must also work in China. Those who do not understand the local culture and simply deploy global policies have had to pay a high price. Those who have understood the issue and integrated cultural difference into their business implementation are reaping the rewards.

Products "Made for China"

It is a mistake to think that there is a global strategy for running a business in China. The localization of products and services is key for global growth and several American and European companies apply it assiduously. They have, as we will see, successfully offered "Made for China" products and services in a market with a culture radically different from their own.

KFC

In 1987, when the first KFC opened in Tiananmen Square, Western-style fast-food restaurants were unknown in China. Many Chinese still wore Mao-era suits and rode bicycles everywhere. KFC was a novelty and a foretaste of American influence. Realizing that in China, as in many other developing countries, food is at the heart of a society, KFC's management adopted a clear and radical strategy to transform the business into a brand that would be perceived as part of Chinese society and would appeal to the masses. Over the years, no matter where it operated, KFC chose locations in the most local and cultural neighborhoods. For example, one of its first restaurants in Beijing was located in an old Qing dynasty-style building where customers could go for a special occasion. Although they didn't initially enjoy the food, they felt at home in this warm and friendly eatery.

KFC executives sought to expand the brand so that Chinese consumers would accept it as part of the local community. They realized that, with food being so central to Chinese society, as it is in many other developing countries, a wide assortment of attractive flavors was essential to appeal to a large number of consumers.

KFC China's menus typically include more than 50 items, compared to approximately 29 in the United States. These items include localized products such as spicy chicken, rice, soymilk drinks, egg pies, fried dough sticks, wraps with local sauces, fish and shrimp burgers on fresh buns, and the popular rice porridge, difficult to prepare at home and now KFC's flagship breakfast offering.

Such variety attracts customers and encourages repeat visits. The company launches approximately 50 new products per year (some are offered temporarily) compared to one or two in the United States. A committee manages a very aggressive strategy on the new product development program.

One of the innovations on KFC's Chinese menu is *chuan*, perhaps its most dissonant brand element. These boiled skewers are a favorite Chinese midnight snack, sold as street food. At one stage, KFC was planning to introduce other snack-style menu items in ten major Chinese cities; it even set up an independent sourcing system for the production of these exclusive items and intended to explore further the sprawling market for midnight snacks in China.

KFC implements the localization strategy in detail. Dishes and spice levels are adjusted for geographic regions where cultures vary. So, consumers in Shanghai are fond of sweet and savory dishes; the Cantonese prefer light dishes and love soups; and the Szechuanese always take their meals with local pepper and chili pepper.

With sustained efforts to establish an American brand with Chinese characteristics, KFC regularly launches innovative dishes that even shock Chinese consumers. However, this policy is paying off. The opening of its largest, three-storey, 500-seat restaurant was an instant success, strategically positioned a stone's throw from Beijing's Tiananmen Square and with customers queuing up outside for months after it opened. By the end of June 2020, with 7,100 restaurants in 1,500 cities, KFC was the country's dominant fast-food player.

Maybelline

Mahjong is a Chinese tile-based board game played by four players, combining tactics, strategy, calculation, psychology and—depending on the regional variations to the rules—a lot of luck. Mahjong is very popular in China and East Asia, especially in Chinese, Japanese, Vietnamese and Thai communities.

For the launch of its new Red On Fire lipstick series during Chinese New Year 2019, Maybelline, a subsidiary of French cosmetics company L'Oréal, created a customized Mahjong set. The traditional symbols on the tiles were replaced by lipsticks and the "New York" icons and Maybelline "M" logo placed on the back. In addition, animation activities were associated with the marketing campaign. For instance, the brand hosted fire-themed pop-up stores in Shenzhen and Tianjin, while a fire truck and Mahjong table were installed for visitors to take selfies.

This launch campaign was a resounding success. Maybelline's Red On Fire collection sold out in mainland China within days. Hundreds of bloggers on China's leading social media platforms talked about it. The keywords "Maybelline Mahjong" flooded search engines as customers tried to find out where to buy the product. A top WeChat fashion blogger said that one of his two favorite items of 2019 was Maybelline's customized Mahjong set. As a result, Maybelline was able to engage influencers and create buzzworthy social awareness for the brand.

While most brands are still struggling to offer products incorporating the Chinese zodiac or traditional Chinese colors, Maybelline has shown that it is capable of connecting deeply with local culture with its custom products.

Decathlon

The Chinese, especially Chinese women, avoid exposure to the sun, learning from their ancestors that too much sun causes sunburn, lesions and skin cancer. The Chinese popularly believe that only farmers are dark-skinned; the rest are light-skinned and fair skin has become an expression of social status. Sunbathing is therefore not part of the Chinese lifestyle. For Chinese women, fair skin resonates with beauty, underscoring the Chinese proverb that "if you have a white skin, it will hide a thousand uglies."

Decathlon achieved resounding success in China with its tents. In fact, one of its surveys revealed the purchasing motivation of their potential customers. Chinese consumers do not buy tents for camping at night but rather use them to protect themselves from the sun during a day at the park. Decathlon's best-selling tent in France is a sturdy, waterproof, two-person tent for overnight camping. Decathlon's best-selling product on China's largest e-commerce platform Tmall is a family tent with light rain protection and UPF 50 sun protection. This tent is not even available in France. If Decathlon had offered the same tents in China as in France, it would have missed the huge market of Chinese families wanting a tent to spend a relaxing day in the park.

Decathlon currently has more than 1,600 stores worldwide and its Chinese website indicated more than 300 stores in the country in early 2021. This number is expected to grow rapidly, some media predicting that a new location will open in China every five days.

IKEA

When IKEA was confronted with the phenomenon of Chinese visitors sleeping on its demonstration beds and hanging out for long hours in its stores, it first tried to combat this behavior by getting its employees to wake up or chase these people away. However, the phenomenon persisted. After some reflection, IKEA decided to embrace Chinese culture and accept this behavior, realizing that sleeping on display furniture was understandable as midday naps are a common habit in China. In addition, it set up chairs in public spaces, such as airports, knowing that Chinese customers would appreciate places to relax.

At first, IKEA China's very high visitor traffic did not convert to sales but the brand remained optimistic, considering that today's visitors could be tomorrow's customers. Chinese attitudes towards shopping are fundamentally different from those in the West. For them, shopping is a form of leisure and entertainment and they interact closely with their business environment.

Today, after 20 years in the Chinese market, IKEA's success is undeniable, with around 30 stores, including seven inaugurated in 2019, and nearly 20,000 employees.

Starbucks

The Starbucks Reserve Roastery in Shanghai, opened on December 6, 2017 on Nanjing Road, is one of the world's largest Starbucks in one of the world's busiest shopping districts, covering approximately 2,700 square meters. By comparison, the Reserve Roastery in Seattle, U.S., covers half this area. The Shanghai Roastery has a number of unique features not found in other Starbucks stores: the longest Starbucks coffee bar, extending 26 meters (88 feet) (a nod is made to the number 88, which symbolizes fortune and good luck in Chinese culture), and a ceiling constructed from 10,000 handmade wooden tiles, with a look "inspired by locking an espresso shot on an espresso machine," according to the company.

Starbucks' success is largely due to its ability to localize its offerings. Working and innovating with local partners and culture are part of its strategy. The Shanghai site uses beans from more than 30 different countries, including from China's Yunnan Province. A Teavana tea bar, the first in China, is built from recycled materials printed in 3D and serves nitrogen-infused tea as well as tea brewed with the Steampunk system which uses steam to extract unique flavors from each tea leaf.

The integration of the latest technology is also part of the services with Chinese characteristics. The Shanghai Roastery is the first Starbucks store to use augmented reality technology. Customers can point their cell phones at various items inside the store to access more information and unlock "virtual badges" to share on social networks.

Starbucks sees China as its largest growth market and continues to expand rapidly. As a result, there were more than 4,800 stores in 200 cities in April 2021. The numbers change constantly as it opens a new location every 15 hours. These success stories of Western companies in China demonstrate how they have managed to localize their products and services through a deep understanding of Chinese culture and a great ability to adapt to the consumer culture of the market.

China is geographically vast and culturally diverse. The localization of products and services in the spirit of "Made for China" needs to be deepened. What works in Shanghai does not necessarily work in Beijing, and what works in big cities almost never works in small towns. Chinese customs and culture vary greatly from region to region, greatly influencing consumer behavior and preferences for products and services. Western companies must strive to understand China region by region and adapt their offerings accordingly.

Communication

To succeed in the Chinese market, Western companies must absolutely "communicate locally". This requires them first to consider the local reality so that they communicate in accordance with local culture and customs and, in particular, to pay close attention to Chinese sensitivity to the local political context.

In November 2018, the Italian company Dolce & Gabbana (D&G) wanted to launch an extensive marketing campaign in China, starting in Shanghai with the biggest fashion show in its history. It began by broadcasting an online advertising video. After a few hours of broadcasting, the video was distributed through Chinese social networks and provoked a strong reaction from internauts who viewed it as racist because of the stereotypical choice of actress, her vulgar, frivolous and submissive attitude, and the ignorant, old-fashioned decor reminiscent of China in the 1970s. Viewers considered the sexual jokes mocking the Chinese race as degrading and labeled the ironic comments about chopsticks as Western arrogance. It almost involved the state. A few days after the incident, CCTV responded by emphasizing the importance of chopsticks to the Chinese people.

D&G suffered a marketing campaign shock. Participants, artists, sponsors and partners withdrew, its Shanghai fashion show was cancelled, and its online stores on e-commerce platforms such as Alibaba and JD were instantly shut down. D&G stores were boycotted; customer returns were massive. Nothing could salvage the situation despite D&G's public apology. Today, three years later, Chinese consumers seem not to have forgiven D&G as its sales in China remain weak.

The D&G case is not isolated. Others have made missteps with catastrophic economic consequences.

In June 2019, Paul Donovan, chief economist of the Swiss bank UBS, was suspended after using the term "Chinese pig" to analyze Chinese inflation in his annual report. This enraged Chinese internauts because "pig" is used in China to connote stupidity and laziness. And in China, associating "pig" or "dog" with a person or a country is an insult.

Haitong International Securities Group, one of China's largest financial institutions, confirmed that it had suspended all collaboration with UBS, while the Securities Association of China called on its members to refrain from quoting from Donovan's report and never to invite him to future events. China Railway Construction Corp. Ltd. excluded UBS from a major bond transaction valued at an estimated USD 1 billion. (56) (57)

Following Chinese demands, Donovan and UBS had to apologize publicly and individually to various Chinese partners before he was reinstated, and the bank stated that it would commit itself to examine future reports more carefully before publishing them, adding that it would ensure that its analysts are trained and sensitized to other cultures and their languages.

In October 2019, Dior made a presentation in China that showed a map of China without Taiwan. Valentino, Swarovski, Zara and Calvin Klein cited Hong Kong and Taiwan as countries separate from China on their websites. Givenchy and Versace sold a T-shirt presenting Hong Kong as a country. They all immediately rectified their errors and officially apologized. (58)

In 2016, the French cosmetics brand Lancôme organized a free promotional concert in Hong Kong (59). A few days later, faced with massive online criticism, it cancelled the concert. The chosen artist, pop singer Denise Ho, had met the Dalai Lama and campaigned for democracy in Hong Kong. Confronted with calls for a Chinese boycott, the luxury brand backed down. Chinese sensitivity to Western support for the Dalai Lama may be offended by a detail. The German car manufacturer Daimler apologized publicly in 2018 after its Mercedes-Benz brand published an ad on Instagram containing a quote from the Dalai Lama.

These incidents illustrate serious problems Western companies face when doing business with China. The Chinese value their country's unity; political problems arising from its history related to Taiwan, Hong Kong or the Dalai Lama are considered as internal affairs and taking these sensitive issues lightly is deemed by the Chinese and their government as a hostile provocation. In order to obtain and maintain access to the Chinese market, Western companies must raise their international awareness to make properly informed business decisions accordingly.

Few Western brands operating in China today can claim to have started their activities in the country more than a century ago. In 1874, the first Western trademark registered in the Hong Kong register belonged to the Swiss group Nestlé.

For a century, Nestlé managers in China have had the power to say no to the Swiss headquarters if a product or marketing campaign is not suitable for the Chinese market. Perhaps the greatest tribute to this strategy is the fact that many Chinese consumers believe that Nestlé is a local company.

In January 2019, Nestlé broadcast a clip entitled "Go Ping Pong" that featured Chinese ping-pong champion Zhang Jike and demonstrated its deep understanding of Chinese culture. The clip described the Chinese father-son relationship with great finesse and concisely chosen and engaging words. Nestlé's sensitivity to Chinese culture moved millions of consumers. In addition to an impeccable narrative, the theme chosen in a communication is also crucial. Chinese consumers react favorably to ads that emphasize family or relationship values rather than pride or personal autonomy.

Chinese consumers' current expectations of Western companies are much more qualitative and behavioral. They receive and interpret corporate communications and immediately comment on social media networks. Reactions often come strong and fast, with radical consequences. Understanding their very different culture, world view and sensitivities, and being able to adapt to them, are essential keys to commercial success in China.

Branding in Chinese

When a foreign company enters the Chinese market, one of its priorities is to find a good Chinese name for its brand, knowing that trademark registration in China follows the principle of "first in, first served".

Foreigners have difficulty pronouncing and remembering Chinese names, and Chinese people also feel uneasy with foreign names. A successful Chinese brand name is the first step to penetrating the Chinese market. Names and their meaning are really important in China. A meaningful name will make a brand much more attractive.

Several parameters must be taken into account when choosing a Chinese name for a foreign brand. The best choice is that which embraces the tone (phonetic translation), meaning (literal translation) and aesthetic appearance of the Chinese characters.

Choosing a phonetic translation of the foreign brand name is particularly beneficial if the foreign brand name already has a reputation in the Chinese market, allowing Chinese consumers to recognize it right away. For example, the Chinese name of the Japan's Sony brand is 索尼, pronounced *Suo Ni* which sounds very much like the original brand name. On the other hand, the translation of these two Chinese characters is "cable" and "Buddhist nun", not particularly consistent with Sony products. There are other examples of foreign brands made according to the same principle: Kraft is pronounced *Ka Fu* in Chinese and written 卡夫; Dior is pronounced *Di Ao* and written 迪奥. None has any meaning in Chinese but all are merely random combinations of characters. Chinese consumers, however, instantly recognize them.

The disadvantage of literal translation is that, in most cases, the sound of a new Chinese name does not resemble the original brand name. Foreign companies will have to spend more time and money on marketing to build brand awareness. Great effort must be made to create the association between the original brand and the Chinese brand. The Apple brand has chosen 苹果 as its Chinese brand—this is the name of the apple fruit in Chinese and is pronounced *Ping Guo* which does not sound like the word "apple". The same happened to Microsoft which adopted 微软 as its Chinese brand. Pronounced *Wei Ruan*, its Chinese name means "soft microphone".

Most foreign companies opt for a combination of the two, integrating phonetic and literal translations. In this way, the Chinese brand sounds more or less the same as the original brand and the chosen Chinese ideograms have a positive meaning from the point of view of Chinese culture. They can resonate as well with its corporate activities or products. The second part of the Mercedes-Benz brand is pronounced *Ben Chi*, written 奔驰, and means "galloping at high speed". The BMW brand is pronounced *Bao Ma*, written 宝马, and means "treasure horse". Nike is pronounced *Nai Ke*, written 耐克, and means "endure and overcome". Canon is pronounced *Jia Neng*, written 佳能, and means "excellent performance".

Any successful marketing strategy starts with a good visual representation of a brand name. There are hundreds of Chinese writing styles. The appearance of the characters includes their visual presentation and choice of font style. The aesthetic appearance of the Chinese characters is the last important touch in choosing a Chinese brand name.

Airbnb

Despite ingenious efforts to find a good Chinese name, some foreign brands still encounter difficulties in the market. Their Chinese brand is not well accepted by the locals. This disrupts their marketing development.

The American home-sharing service Airbnb has opted for a Chinese name pronounced *Aibiying*, written 爱彼迎, and means "to welcome each other with love". At first glance, it seems well chosen: Its tonality is close to the original brand and the meaning of the chosen brand name is in line with the company's activities. But Chinese consumers find it difficult to pronounce the two syllables with similar juxtaposed sounds. Culturally speaking, it sounds like they are saying "like to meet demands". A Chinese internaut commented, "I feel uncomfortable putting the Airbnb application icon with others because it could be seen as a sex-related product application at a quick glance."

Coca-Cola

For the Chinese, the Golden Palm award goes to the American brand Coca-Cola for its realization of their Chinese brand name. Pronounced *Ke Kou Ke Le*, it is written 可口可乐 and means "good for the mouth, good for happiness". The Chinese characters signifying three symbols of an open mouth ready to taste delight the Chinese people.

Yet, when Coca-Cola sought to enter the Chinese market in 1930, its Chinese name was difficult to pronounce and meaningless. The company then placed an ad in *The Times* newspaper in London and organized a competition to find a better name. Jiang Yi, a Chinese writer and poet, won the contest and created the name we know today. The winner's prize was £350. The story became an inspiring and popular anecdote.

Some foreign companies argue that their original brand is a perfect embodiment of their identity. They want to communicate their foreign character to Chinese consumers and are reluctant to adopt a Chinese name. This mindset ignores cultural differences and the benefits that could be derived from adapting to local consumer preferences. A Chinese-language brand can very well become the local embodiment of the culture, values, personality and vision of the foreign brand. It merely requires some ingenuity and creativity.

The choice of location

Choosing a location to set up a company or commercial unit is one of the most strategic and decisive steps in a business project. Regardless of the target country, a long list of parameters is taken into consideration. The Chinese market is no exception. The population of the cities, their economic and educational level, installation costs, infrastructure and local government regulations must be studied meticulously. A high degree of adaptability in the strategic planning of the choice of location is required.

China is not a homogeneous market. Each region has different economic, demographic and cultural characteristics. Identifying the opportunities and challenges in each region is critical to succeed in this market. Understanding Chinese cultural influences in the classification, organization and new development of its cities is a key asset.

Tier system

A hierarchical system is fundamental to Chinese society, manifested in the structure of the family and in social and professional relationships. The unofficial classification of Chinese cities is also an obvious illustration of this system.

Given the rapid development of Chinese cities and their constant dynamic evolution, a tier classification system with Chinese characteristics has gained great popularity in recent years and become an indispensable reference in strategic business planning.

The Chinese city tier system is a hierarchical classification. There are no such official lists in China since the Chinese government does not publish or recognize such an official definition. However, it is frequently mentioned in various media publications, including the state media. All economists, consultants and companies frequently refer to the tier system when choosing a location or developing a marketing strategy. The Chinese population uses it to assess the standard of living or the situation of business, transportation, tourism and education.

Given the considerable number of cities in China and the speed at which new cities are formed, there is no single version of this classification. China's 600 cities are conventionally divided into four tiers and the popular consensus is that four cities belong to Tier 1: Beijing (one of the world's megacities), Shanghai, Guangzhou and Shenzhen. They are colloquially known as "Bei-Shang-Guang-Shen". Tier-1 cities represent the most developed areas of the country with the most affluent and sophisticated consumers. They are large, densely populated urban metropolises that have enormous economic, cultural and political influence in China. Being able to live and work in Tier-1 cities is considered prestigious by many Chinese living inland.

Different organizations define the tiers by using a number of factors, two in particular: GDP and population. All cities in Tier 1 have a GDP of more than USD 300 billion; Tier 2 a GDP between USD 68 and 299 billion; Tier 3 a GDP between USD 18 and 67 billion; and Tier 4 a GDP of less than USD 17 billion. Tier-1 cities have more than 15 million inhabitants; Tier 2 between three and 15 million; Tier 3 between 150,000 and three million; and Tier 4 fewer than 150,000. (60)

This means that China cannot be treated as a single market. Consumers in different regions and cities have very different income levels, behaviors and trends. Cities in different tiers vary considerably in population size, consumer preference, infrastructure, level of sophistication of products and services, talent resource and business opportunities. The tier system derived from Chinese culture provides a handy and direct way to deciphering this complex information.

Cluster system

Chinese society is strongly influenced by Confucianism, which advocates collectivism. This influence manifests itself in all fields, including the way of organizing the development of China's industries.

The history of Chinese industrial consolidation dates back to the 1950s. China began consolidating its domestic industries on the instructions of Chairman Mao Zedong during the Cold War era. The Chinese feared Soviet or American attacks on cities such as Beijing and Shanghai. As a result, strategic industries were regrouped and spread throughout the country.

China today uses an inherited system of industrial clustering to balance economic development, encouraging Chinese companies from different industries to set up and work together in specific regions and cities. In some industries, most supply chains may exist in a small localized area.

Knowing where these industry clusters are located can help Western companies determine where their target customers, human resources or supply chains are located so they can make a better decision on their own location.

The Chinese government defined 19 city clusters in its 13th Five-Year Plan (2016–2020). Three of these clusters—Pearl River Delta (PRD), Yangzi River Delta (YRD) and Bohai Rim (Beijing-Tianjin-Hebei)—are world class and the most innovative and internationally competitive. The majority of these clusters are located in the eastern provinces of Jiangsu, Zhejiang, Fujian and Guangdong. The Yangzi Midstream cluster in central China and the Chengdu-Chongqing cluster in southwest China will soon join the ranks of the three world-class clusters due to their rapid development.

Among many industry divisions, the main business clusters in China are agriculture, high-tech and manufacturing. Modern agricultural clusters are developing mainly around Beijing and the provinces of Shandong and Shanxi. Among them is Shouguang vegetable cluster in Shandong province. Shouguang is the hometown of Jia Sixie, 6th-century author of the world's first agricultural encyclopedia *Qi Min Yao Shu*. A pilot cluster during the Rural Reform, Shouguang covers an area of about 32,000 square kilometers and produces about three billion kilograms of vegetables annually to feed more than half of the country. One of China's biggest vegetable exporters, it is today internationally famous as the "home of Chinese vegetables". (61)

Another example is Jinxiang garlic cluster in Shandong province. Garlic has been cultivated in Jinxiang County for more than 2,000 years; the cluster produces an average of 800,000 tons annually and has a storage capacity of two million tons. It exports 70% of total Chinese garlic production to more than 160 countries and regions. (62)

With the development and changing structure of agriculture, agro-industry clusters have started to emerge in many parts of China. These include the Anxi tea cluster (Fujian province), the Chenggong flower cluster (Yunnan province) and the Guixian sugar cluster (Guangxi province).

China's five high-tech pioneers are Beijing, Shenzhen, Hangzhou, Guangzhou and Chengdu, leading the country's technological innovation and shaping the future of high-tech in the world. Beijing is the richest source of unicorns, privately held start-ups valued at more than USD 1 billion; Hangzhou is the capital of the e-commerce industry; and Shenzhen sets the benchmark for technological manufacturing.

Different from the phenomenon that is Silicon Valley in the U.S., China's technological poles are spread over many megacities with strong economies and deep talent pools. E-commerce company JD.com, vehicle-for-hire leader DiDi and internet giant Baidu, Inc. all have their headquarters in Beijing. Zhongguancun technology hub is located in Haidian District, a prestigious university district in northern Beijing.

Home to the headquarters of world Internet industry leaders such as the Alibaba Group, Hangzhou, which has earned the title of "China's E-commerce capital", forms with Shanghai the Yangzi River Delta Economic Zone, one of China's most dynamic and innovative clusters, and is an emerging hub of blockchain technology after the opening in April 2018 of the Hangzhou Blockchain Industrial Park.

Alpha city Shenzhen, China's first Special Economic Zone, is a gleaming embodiment of the country's economic acceleration and attracts many investors. With currently more than three million companies, R&D investment will continue to be one of the highest in the world. As part of the Greater Bay Area (GBA), the richest and largest economic region in South China, Shenzhen is a leading global technology and R&D hub, high-tech equipment and robotics manufacturer (it is the headquarters of companies such as Huawei, Tencent and ZTE), and a magnet for tourism.

Guangzhou, also in the GBA, is another Alpha city brimming with international trade and is at the forefront of high-tech innovation in the country. One of China's busiest ports, it benefits from its proximity to Shenzhen and Hong Kong and has become a hub for international transport.

Chengdu, in the province of Sichuan in Southwest China, is part of the Chengdu-Chongqing city cluster which is one of the privileged corridors of the BRI and is expected to become the fourth pillar of China's economy, after the Yangzi River Delta, Pearl River Delta and Beijing-Tianjin-Hebei regions. It will be China's inland economic engine. By expanding internationally and integrating global industrial networks, Chengdu has become the fourth-largest IT industry hub in China, after Beijing, Shanghai and Guangzhou. A long-established base for the electronics and IT industries, the city has developed into the global center for the telecom, high technology and R&D industries. Chengdu is a magnet for a variety of multinational companies, including Nokia, Microsoft, IBM and Cisco, but aims to become a hub for start-ups and plans to produce at least seven unicorns by 2022.

China manufactures everything under the sun. It is known as "the world's factory" because of its strong business ecosystem, cheap and abundant labor, raw materials, and relaxed regulatory compliance. This manufacturing powerhouse is dotted with manufacturing clusters, some more recognized than others as leaders in their industry. The list below provides an overview of these industries and their main geographical distributions:

Electronics: the Guangdong region
Textiles: Zhejiang, Jiangsu

Leathers and feathers: southeast coastal areas

Metal products: Zhejiang, Guangdong, Jiangsu, Shandong, Hebei, Henan

Glass: Hebei, Jiangsu

Ceramics: Jingdezhen in the province of Jiangxi

Furniture: Guangdong and Hebei

Construction: Shandong

Household appliances: Guangdong, Zhejiang, Shandong

Artware & sport: Zhejiang, Fujian, Guangdong, Hubei

Papermaking and printing: Guangdong, Zhejiang, Jiangsu, Shandong, Fujian

Machinery: Dongbei region, Hunan and Hubei provinces

Petrochemicals: Shandong, Liaoning, Guangdong

Pharmaceuticals: Tianjin city, Xian city in Shanxi province

Food and beverages: Liaoning, Shandong, Jiangsu, Guangdong, Fujian, Hebei, Henan, Hunan, Hubei, Inner Mongolia

Motorcars and bicycles: Taizhou city in Zhejiang province

Shipping: Yangzi River Delta, Pearl River Delta, Bohai Bay area

Automotive: Jilin, Hubei, Shanghai, Beijing, the Pearl River Delta

Free-Trade Zones (FTZs)

Chinese philosophy has played a fundamental role in China's objective of promoting and leading the development of an unprecedented degree of economic openness. The opening of the Chinese economy to the world is the result of a strong will for increasing economic development. This is obvious to all. Few people see its cultural DNA. Chinese philosophy plays a fundamental role in the speed and power of this will to embrace and integrate the Western economy. The Taoist notion of duality is expressed in the concept of yin and yang, i.e., "black-white", "positive-negative", and drives the Chinese to see the West as yang and China as yin. The two energies are opposed but complementary. To achieve ultimate success, these two energies must be in a state of equilibrium. Chinese companies need the knowledge and strengths of Western companies, so China's natural goal is to secure long-term cooperation with them.

China launched its first pilot free-trade zones (FTZ) in Shanghai in 2013. These FTZs were designed as testing grounds for a number of economic and social reforms and their introduction in a single and tightly controlled region allowed new economic, tax and regulatory practices to be tested and developed before considering expansion nationally. The aim is to integrate the international economy into the Chinese economy by getting increasingly inspired from international practices.

An FTZ can be defined as a geographical region within a country which is subject to special economic laws that are less restrictive than those governing the rest of the country, and where importers and manufacturers are afforded exceptionally favorable conditions and are exempt from particular customs duties, regulations, etc.

They offer many advantages to foreign companies by facilitating access to markets, cross-border trade, setups and investments. It is becoming increasingly easier for foreign companies to enter the Chinese market through FTZs which offer many advantages to companies looking to export to China. Import regulations and processes are simplified, import taxes are low, company registrations are fast, and bonded warehouses are available. Goods can move between Chinese FTZs and abroad, free of taxes and duties.

Companies registered under the Chinese WFOE law enjoy numerous advantages, including the ability to sell products and services directly to the Chinese market, hire Chinese employees, issue tax receipts, take advantage of income tax reductions, benefit from reduced or non-existent foreign exchange controls, and easily manage foreign exchange conversions.

Since 2013, China has expanded its FTZs to other coastal regions, such as Guangdong, Tianjin, Fujian, Zhejiang, Liaoning and Hainan, and to inland regions, such as Henan, Hubei, Sichuan and Shaanxi. In August 2019, following the confirmed success, the development of the FTZs was accelerated and six additional zones were installed, respectively in Jiangsu, Shandong, Hebei, Heilongjiang, Guanxi and Yunnan.

Seeking greater openness and high-quality development, China in September 2020 officially opened three new FTZs in Beijing, Anhui and Hunan provinces and one expanded zone in Zhejiang province, bringing the total number of FTZs in the country to 21 and demonstrating its determination to accelerate the formation of an economic development model through ever-increasing openness.

FTZ locations are not chosen randomly but rather according to a strategic, long-term plan that covers specific objectives and different industries to improve connectivity and collaboration with neighboring regions.

The new Beijing pilot FTZ focuses on building an international innovation center. The construction of a zone for the expansion of trade in services and a pilot zone for the digital economy will be realized.

The Hunan FTZ is focusing on building a manufacturing cluster. It represents an investment and trade corridor connecting the Yangzi River Economic Zone and the Guangdong-Hong Kong-Macao GBA. It also serves as a leading region for deep economic and trade cooperation between China and Africa.

Located inland, the An Hui FTZ focuses on promoting the deep integration of scientific and technological innovation and economic development. It accelerates the development of manufacturing clusters in strategic emerging industries and promotes the integrated development of the Yangzi River Delta and its surrounding region.

The expanded Zhejiang FTZ is focusing on the construction of a new type of international trade center and a global shipping and logistics center, as well as the construction of a raw material resource allocation base centered on oil and gas. It is also carrying out the construction of a digital economy development demonstration zone and a cluster zone for advanced manufacturing industries.

Chinese character according to regions

Understanding Chinese culture in business implementation is inseparable from human contact. Foreign companies need to interact closely with their Chinese suppliers, customers, partners and employees.

Though Europe is renowned for its cultural diversity, the French, Germans and Italians do not share the same characteristics. The Romance, Germanic and Slavic cultures are distinct from one another, with each population enjoying a specific reputation. Prejudices and misunderstandings are frequent, and both also exist among Chinese in different regions to create daily difficulties in interpersonal communication.

With hugely diverse geographical environments, climates, histories and cultures, each region in China has its own dialect, eating habits and lifestyle. All of these factors have shaped regional personalities and mentalities so that when one Chinese meets another for the first time, they reflexively ask, "where are you from?"

Beijing

Beijing has for several centuries been the capital of China and its political, economic and cultural center. The Forbidden City, Summer Palace, Temple of Heaven, Ming Tombs and the Great Wall can be seen here. Beijing symbolizes the fusion of Chinese tradition and modernity—its modernity is represented by the National Stadium, aka the Bird's Nest, the National Aquatic Center, aka the Water Cube, the Great National Theater, the National Library of China, the National Museum and the CCTV headquarters.

The Mandarin spoken by the Pekingese is considered the national standard. More than 92% of Chinese speak Mandarin, but many speak with an accent from their region. Each Chinese region, province or city has its own dialect and people from the same place speak the dialect among themselves.

The Pekingese have a reputation for being bold, loyal, diplomatic, elegant, hospitable and having a sense of humor. Chinese from other regions sometimes reproach the Pekingese for excessive obedience and cunning, probably because of having lived "at the feet" of emperors for centuries.

Shanghai

With 24 million inhabitants, Shanghai is the largest city in China. Located on the southern estuary of the Yangzi River, it is the country's economic, financial, commercial, industrial, technological and transportation heartbeat. This China showpiece is renowned for its breathtaking skyline, architectural styles, and the most impressive exhibitions.

The Shanghainese have a reputation for being astute, meticulous, conscientious and business-savvy. Shanghainese women are often complimented for their gentleness and perspicacity. According to the Chinese of other regions, the Shanghainese can be conceited and calculating.

Tianjin

Tianjin, one of China's four municipalities, is the largest port in Northern China located mainly along the Hai River at the confluence of the Yellow River (Huang He) and the Yangzi River via the Grand Canal. It is also located on the shores of the Gulf of Bohai.

The city is home to the first museum of the Great Wall, the Memorial to Zhou Enlai (the PRC's first premier under Mao Zedong) and Deng Yingchao (Zhou Enlai's wife), the Temple of Great Compassion, St. Joseph Cathedral in the former French concession, and the Cathedral of Notre Dame des Victoires. Tianjin's new Binhai economic zone has been called "the third growth pole of China".

The people of Tianjin are often described as being optimistic and philosophical, with a good sense of humor, although they can be unambitious and gluttonous.

Chongqing

Chongqing is one of the four Chinese municipalities directly administered by the central government. Located deep inland in the southwestern part of the country on the upper reaches of the Yangzi River, it is the region's political, economic and cultural center.

Chongqing has a notoriously hot and subtropical monsoon climate, making it one of the "Three Furnaces" of China's Yangzi River Valley. Built on a mountainous promontory, it is known as a "mountain city" and nicknamed "Fog Capital" because of the thick fog that enshrouds it in winter and spring.

The people of Chongqing have a reputation for being warm, outgoing, enthusiastic, a little rustic and simple. It is said that the native Chinese of this region have a sense of justice, hard work and humor, but are also angry, emotional and impatient.

Dongbei

Culturally diverse Northeastern China, known by its Chinese name as Dongbei, comprises the provinces of Heilongjiang, Jilin and Liaoning. Its inhabitants the Tungus have cultural similarities with their Korean and Japanese neighbors. With Inner Mongolia neighboring this region, Dongbei cuisine has a strong Korean and Mongolian influence. It has the highest concentration of Russians, one of the minorities officially recognized by the Chinese government. Dongbei is also steeped in the Manchu culture.

Benefiting from rich carboniferous resources, the region was industrialized under the Japanese occupation. It is one of the most important industrial regions in China.

While its summers are hot and dry, its winters are bitterly cold. Its inhabitants are physically taller and larger than the Chinese average and are known for their courage, generosity and extrovert nature. They are also considered to be thoughtless daredevils.

Shandong

Located in East China in the lower reaches of the Yellow River, Shandong, the birthplace of Confucius, is one of China's most populous provinces. The centuries-old Grand Canal, a UNESCO World Heritage Site, passes through Shandong. Considered the cradle of Chinese civilization, the city has for centuries been one of the most developed centers of agriculture and handicrafts.

Shandong's inhabitants are generally robustly built with a strong voice. They have a reputation for being simple, warm, caring and filial. However, they are regularly criticized by their compatriots for being rude, unrestrained, and prone to alcohol and eating too much meat.

Jiangzhe

Jiangzhe is a region in the east of China that includes two provinces: Jiangsu and Zhejiang.

Jiangsu is an eastern-central coastal province of China and the country's most densely populated. It borders the Yellow Sea and the Yangtze River cuts through the south. A very wealthy province with one of China's highest GDPs, Jiangsu has a rich historical and cultural past especially visible in its two most important cities, Nanjing and Suzhou, that are centers of education, research, politics, transportation and tourism. Suzhou is particularly famous for its centuries-old silk production. Suzhou is famous for the quality of its silk, its meticulously designed gardens, and its criss-crossing network of canals.

Zhejiang province borders Jiangsu to the south and is similarly wealthy after a spectacular post-Mao economic revival. Its capital city Hangzhou was the original 12th-century capital of the Southern Song dynasty and is the southern terminus of the Grand Canal, a UNESCO World Heritage site. Hangzhou has developed an extremely broad range of industries and is the headquarters of the Alibaba Group. The capital of Zhejiang, was chosen as the capital of the Southern Song dynasty because of its beauty. This ancient city, built on the shores of the famous Western Lake, has a rich architectural heritage and attracts many tourists.

According to an ancient Chinese poem, which encapsulates the beauty of these two cities, "In heaven there is paradise; on earth there is Suzhou and Hangzhou". The Jiangzhe region is also considered the cradle and origin of Chinese civilization

The people of these two provinces are described as cultivated, intelligent, gentle and stable, but with two defects: complicated and anxious.

Guangdong

Guangdong, one of China's most prosperous provinces, is located on the north shore of the South China Sea, bordering Hong Kong. The region is the ancestral home for many Overseas Chinese involved as laborers in railway construction in North America in the 19th century. As a result, many of today's Overseas Chinese have their roots in this province. The Cantonese were the first to be influenced by foreigners and in particular by modern Western cultural thinking. With this openness, Guangdong has nurtured a generation of democratic political pioneers in modern China, among them Kang Youwei, Liang Qichao and Sun Yat-sen (the acknowledged founder of the first republic).

Guangdong is the cradle of the Lingnan culture famous for its Cantonese cuisine that features well-balanced, light and varied ingredients at the peak of their freshness and quality. Lingnan people are known for their pragmatism, open-mindedness, indulgence and innovative ability but northern Chinese sometimes reproach the Cantonese for being too realistic and greedy.

Inner Mongolia

The Inner Mongolia Autonomous Region, the birthplace of Genghis Khan and the holy land of people on horseback, is an enormous elongated region located in northern China and covered by the Gobi Desert. Rich in large reserves of coal, iron ore and rare-earth elements, Inner Mongolia has the world's largest rare-earth mine.

Throughout its history, what is now Inner Mongolia was controlled by southern Chinese farmers and Xiongnu nomads. Cereal cultivation, animal husbandry, forestry and hunting are important economic activities in the region.

Mongols have a sturdy body, broad face, wide ears, bright eyes, prominent cheekbones, curly hair, strong voice and muscular arms. They have a reputation for being brave, loyal and kind but have been criticized for being brutal, rough and tough. In China, they are called "prairie eagles".

Qinghai

Qinghai, located at high altitude in northwest China, is the country's fourth-largest province in area. Its name is taken from colossal Qinghai Lake, China's largest saltwater lake which stands on the "Roof of the World", the Tibetan Plateau.

Adjacent to Tibet, Xinjiang, Gansu and Sichuan, the province is home to different ethnic groups such as Tibetans, Mongols, Uyghurs, Hui Muslims, Salars and Hans. Grass thrives in this region—it possesses some of China's best pasturelands for sheep, horses and yaks. Yak milk tea is a popular local specialty.

The people of Qinghai are known for their righteousness, joie de vivre and hospitality but also for their lack of hygiene—the region's sparse water supply and drought do not allow for frequent showers.

***

China has made giant strides in recent years to adapt to Western culture and conform to existing international economic standards. The Chinese business culture is beginning to change, as Chinese companies are increasingly adopting a global approach and international perception. The two cultures have come closer together in the dynamics of globalization.

There will undoubtedly always be a significant gap of understanding to be bridged between Chinese and Western culture. Although it will take some time to narrow or even eliminate this gap, it is very important that Western companies understand it and participate in bridging it because a 5,000-year-old culture does not change overnight. Learning how to manage the Chinese cultural aspect in business implementation makes for an effective and ultimately successful strategy.

Chinese business etiquette

Despite the current international challenges, the world is more globalized than ever before and China's onward economic march unstoppable.

Western companies are ahead of their Chinese counterparts in many areas and more than a century of industrial achievement and economic know-how ensures that their products and services always appeal to Chinese consumers. However, a well-planned business strategy and substantial financial investments are not enough to conquer the Chinese market; it is essential that Western companies build trust with their Chinese counterparts from the get-go, thoroughly immersing themselves in Chinese cultural practices and business etiquette.

Rituals constitute an important part of China's culture. Throughout history, ancient rituals have evolved and been integrated and simplified in Chinese society. In ancient times, its ritual system consisted of "Five Rites" applied in distinct social encounters. *Ji li* (auspicious rites) were mainly offerings and sacrifices to heaven, earth and various spirits; *jia li* were congratulatory rites for various festivities, especially marriage;

bin li were hosting rites for greeting guests; *jun li* involved a range of military ceremonies; and *xiong li* (funeral rites) were mainly for mourning. *The Book of Rites*, or *Liji*, a collection of Confucian texts that describe ceremonial rites of the Zhou dynasty, has been passed down through the generations to emphasize social responsibility embodied in good form, decorum and politeness.

Respect for rituals is a cherished component of Chinese daily life, whether in public or in private, and is indispensable to business relationships. It is no surprise that China calls itself "a state of courtesy and ritual".

Greetings

For Westerners, it's useful to have an overview of Chinese hospitality practices. The Chinese traditionally greet each other without touching. The ancient and complex gestures of greeting have gradually been abandoned, replaced by a simplified gesture commonly practiced today. It involves clasping one hand over a closed fist in front of the chest. Women place the right hand over the left; men place the left hand over the right. The position of the hands is reversed only during mourning ceremonies. The height of the gesture determines the degree of respect: the higher the gesture, the greater the respect—but never higher than the head.

Today, however, handshakes are widely practiced in China. During a meeting between a Westerner and a Chinese, it is recommended that the Westerner wait for their Chinese counterpart to offer their hand first. Handshakes should not be too firm; it could be considered aggressive.

Courtesy titles are systematically applied. As a sign of respect, people receive a title followed by their last name, both in private and business relationships. For example: Doctor Li, Professor Zhang, Engineer Wang, Lawyer Liu, Master Huang, etc.

It is common to call a person of the same age or older by their name, preceded by the word "teacher" even if that person is not actually a teacher. It is simply a sign of respect to acknowledge that the other person is more knowledgeable than oneself. The Chinese regard humility as a virtue in social relations. To explicitly acknowledge a compliment, for example, would offend their cultural heritage and the Confucian teachings on humility and modesty.

Giving out business cards during a business meeting is a solemn ritual. The card must be presented with both hands, with the legible side facing the recipient so they can read it. The head should be slightly lowered in respect; the lower the head is tilted forward, the greater the respect shown. However, this should not be exaggerated. After receiving the business card in return, it should be carefully examined and the content repeated if necessary, to underline the admiration of the person's expertise. Acknowledging a Chinese person's high position in a company indicates that you have taken the time to look at their business card and notice their importance as a sign of respect for authority.

It is advisable for a Western professional to have their business card translated into Chinese to signify acceptance and appreciation of Chinese culture. Acquiring a name in Chinese is an art and the same factors relating to the business brand apply. Chinese names are traditionally written with the family name preceding the first name. Married women keep their maiden name, except in rare cases.

There is a cultural taboo regarding where to place the business card after the reception. It is not advisable to place it in a trouser or skirt pocket, as this may imply that the recipient is sitting on the giver. It could suggest a lack of respect or even insolence. This unwritten rule is also valid if the business card has been previously put away in a wallet. The card should be placed in front of the recipient, clearly visible during the meeting, or in the chest pocket, which the Chinese could interpret as a symbol of kindness and friendship.

When Western and Chinese delegations meet, warm applause is appropriate as a sign of honor. Westerners should simply applaud back.

When welcoming visitors from abroad, especially for the first time, the Chinese hosts routinely send a representative of the same hierarchical level as the visitors to meet them at the airport and accompany them to the hotel. Depending on the context, people in the higher or lower hierarchy may perform this task. This may reflect the importance that the host wishes to place on visitors.

Symbolism

In business everywhere, first impressions count, but especially in China where its culture is rich in symbolism. The Chinese attach great importance not only to the forms of gestures and names but also to gifts, colors and numbers. Moreover, the symbolism attached to the mythical dragon is literally opposite to that attached to it in the West.

Gifts

Offering gifts to Chinese clients, colleagues or partners is a ritualistic art worthy of a separate book. Nevertheless, some basic rules deserve to be emphasized because they differ fundamentally from those observed in the West.

The offering of gifts is guided by deeply rooted principles. The Chinese, particularly the elderly, generally do not immediately accept a gift—they repeatedly decline it before accepting it. One should therefore gently insist, while being sensitive to real refusals.

Nor do the Chinese usually open gifts right away unless the giver insists. This custom is slowly beginning to fade among the younger generations who are increasingly westernized and more spontaneous.

Accepting a gift is like that of a business card: receive it with both hands, with the head tilted slightly forward.

Respect for the elderly is a closely guarded moral rule in China. Older people should in general receive a better gift than younger people, or at least a gift perceived as having a higher value.

In the West, we often express our thanks for a gift by sending a card but in China the appropriate expression of thanks is to offer another gift in return. The rule of reciprocity is a ritual followed in Chinese relational interaction. A favor received is a favor returned.

In Chinese culture, people value the symbolism of a gift more than the gift itself. A gift carries a message. Particular attention must therefore be paid to cultural taboos; to ignore them can be perceived as a serious offense. Cultural taboos can be linked to different things: the tone of words, history, anecdote and tradition. In a society that cherishes gatherings and unity, many words are associated with unfortunate or sad events and you ignore the cultural taboos surrounding gifts at your peril.

The Chinese avoid gifting clocks. The word "clock" and the act of "giving a clock" are pronounced like *Zhong* and *Song Zhong* which coincide with "mourning" and "accompany mourning". So, clocks are unlucky gifts.

The Chinese word for "umbrella" sounds like the word "scattered", so gifting an umbrella symbolizes the breaking of a relationship. Giving an umbrella to a married couple suggests a wish for divorce. On the other hand, it is perfectly appropriate to give someone an umbrella if it's raining.

A gift of fruit is fine, but not pears because the Chinese word for "pear" sounds like the word for "separated".

Be careful not to gift shoes because the Chinese word for "shoe" sounds the same as the word for "misfortune".

When it comes to men, gifting a green hat signals that a man's wife or girlfriend has been unfaithful to him. The origin of this taboo is an anecdote about the wife of a merchant in ancient China who had an affair with a clothier. She made a green hat for her husband. When the husband was away on business, she insisted that he wear the hat, which would alert the clothier that he could meet his lover. Green hats have since become a symbol of female infidelity.

Sharp objects, such as knives or scissors, are considered aggressive objects in social relationships. According to a common Chinese saying, "a single knife stab produces two cut pieces", so sharp objects are metaphors for severing a relationship or friendship.

Flowers are naturally a lovely gift but in China some types are generally used for funerals. Chrysanthemums and white flowers are especially taboo because they are used to remember the deceased and are placed on graves.

Candles are similarly associated with rituals for the deceased.

Speaking of mourning, there is one trick worth noting. A common gift for bereavement can be a red envelope containing cash. The Chinese are pragmatic. Cash is viewed as a way to express condolences and contribute to funeral expenses, whereas a cash gift in a red envelope for birthdays or weddings is received as a wish for success. In all cases, though, handing over cash directly as a gift is prohibited.

Offering gifts in China plays a key role in society and especially in business. The Chinese generally spend a high percentage of their budget on buying gifts and, when traveling abroad, Chinese tourists can, according to some statistics, spend up to 90% of their budget on buying gifts for their relatives or business relations. It is a Chinese social requirement.

Colors

China is a country rich in cultural heritage. Colors have had a special symbolism for centuries and are carefully selected when used for ceremonies, festivals and rituals.

According to Chinese tradition, colors are intimately linked with the Five Elements Theory that describes interactions and relationships between things. The five elements— metal, wood, water, fire, earth —are believed to be the fundamental elements of everything in the universe between which interactions occur. The colors of metal are white, gold and silver; the colors of wood are green, cyan and emerald green; the colors of water are black, blue and gray; the colors of fire are red and purple; and the colors of earth are yellow and brown.

In China, the color red, representing fire, is the most popular and beloved color, symbolizing happiness, beauty, vitality, luck, success and good fortune. Red is widely used for traditional celebrations (brides traditionally wear red), private and corporate events (cash is distributed in small red envelopes), and for interior and exterior decorations.

Black is a solemn color. In the *Book of Changes (Yi Jing)*, among the oldest of Chinese texts, black is considered the color of heaven and is associated with symbolizing the northern direction, as the northern skies appeared black to the Chinese. They interpreted the North Star as the emperor of the sky, so black became the king of colors. The symbol for *taiji* uses black and white to represent "the unity of yin and yang, of heaven and man on earth". Black also represents darkness, the unknown and fear.

In traditional Chinese culture, white is the opposite of red and is associated with the lack of blood or absence of life, hence it is associated with winter, death and mourning at funerals. The ancient Chinese wore white clothes and hats when mourning the deceased, a tradition that continues today, especially in rural areas.

Since white and black are associated with mourning and sorrow, during joyful celebrations, gifts, their wrapping and other objects should not be predominantly black or white.

In ancient times, yellow was the most important color to the Chinese, symbolizing royalty, power and prestige. The country's first emperor was called the "Yellow Emperor". China is called the "Yellow Land" and its "mother river" is the Yellow River. The color was long reserved for the emperor. During the Song dynasty (960–1279), glazed yellow tiles were used to build imperial palaces. During the Ming (1368–1644) and Qing (1645–1911) dynasties, emperors were dressed in yellow imperial robes. They were carried in "yellow palace" palanquins and walked along "yellow paths". The official imperial flags were yellow and the official imperial seals wrapped in yellow cloth. Overlooking the Forbidden City, Beijing's Jing Mountain offers a view of a sea of yellow glazed tile roofs. In Chinese Buddhism, yellow is associated with liberation from material needs and monks wear yellow robes.

One notable exception: The color yellow is pronounced *huang* in Chinese and in modern China this word is also used to describe pornography. Its origin dates back to the beginning of the 20th century when an American newspaper published daring drawings on yellow paper to save its business.

Numbers

In Chinese culture, most numbers have a special meaning. For example, 2, 6, 8 and 9 are considered favorable, while 4 is considered unfavorable.

Chinese numerology regards pairs as favorable, so the number 2 is most often considered to be a good number. There is a Chinese saying that "good things come in pairs". It is common to repeat characters to have a stronger effect. The character 喜 means "happiness" but, when repeated, 囍, it means "double happiness".

The Chinese word for "death" phonetically resembles the number 4, hence its negative association with bad luck. People can go to extremes based on superstition to avoid the number 4. Most public facilities avoid it; buildings, their addresses, and their elevators don't contain it, and people prefer to avoid it in identification numbers, telephone numbers, license plates and product names. Houses and apartments with the number 4 in their address fetch much lower prices. Mentioning the number 4 to a sick person could be considered offensive.

Lucky number 6, pronounced *liu*, sounds like the word that means "to flow", which jibes with the popular Chinese idiom *liu liu da shun*, meaning "everything flows smoothly". Multiples of 6 are appreciated.

The Chinese are obsessed with the number 8 because it sounds the same as the word meaning "prosperity". So, the number 8 is associated with wealth, success and good fortune. Multiples of 8 are even more appreciated. An 8th-floor apartment is the most coveted. An address with the number 8 will be considered lucky. License plates and mobile numbers containing the number 8 fetch higher prices. In 2014, two license plates with the number "8888" were sold separately for RMB 12 million and RMB 17.2 million in Zhengzhou and Shenzhen. Many airlines use combinations of the number 8 as flight numbers. Couples prefer to associate this number with their babies. In 2008, there were 170 million newborns, five million more than in 2007, a record since the early 1990s. Most babies were born around August; parents hoped the eighth month would bring fortune to their children. But perhaps the best example of the Chinese love for number 8 is the 2008 Beijing Olympics. The opening ceremony started exactly at eight minutes and eight seconds after 8 p.m. on August 8, the eighth month of the eighth year of the 21st century. This choice expressed the national wish to win the most in the games and to garner success for the country.

The number 9 is pronounced exactly like the Chinese words for "sustainable" and "eternity". It represents longevity on birthdays and weddings. The number 9 was traditionally associated with power and the emperor, whose robes were adorned with nine dragons. During their daily meeting with the emperor, officials were assigned seats organized in nine rows.

And the Forbidden City palace complex is said to have 9,999 rooms.

In recent years, the Chinese have also been inventing numeronyms to create slang, an invention also adopted in business practices. Series of numbers are used to represent words. Thus, 520 is used to say "I love you" and people sometimes use it in text messages. The number 1314 represents the Chinese for "one life, one world" to declare an everlasting promise. This is often combined with 520 to get 521314 which represents "I love you forever"; 555, pronounced *wuwuwu*, represents the sound of crying; 250 means "idiot" or "stupid person".

Every culture has its superstitions and beliefs about numbers. Chinese superstitions reflect their strong belief in invisible forces. The force of "heaven" is the central value of Taoist philosophy, according to which humanity's ultimate destiny is to borrow the invisible force of "heaven" in order to attain "the unity of heaven and man on earth". In any business setting, the importance of numbers toy the Chinese should be taken seriously.

Dragon

The Chinese dragon is a far different mythological beast from its Western counterpart. The Western dragon is a winged, sharp-clawed, scaly-skinned, fire-breathing, cave-dwelling creature routinely associated with evil. Christianity renders the dragon the symbol of evil, the beast in the Book of Revelation (also known as the Apocalypse of John), the incarnation of Satan and paganism. The Book of Revelation describes the dragon's fight against Michael. In the *Golden Legend*, the stories of the holy dragon slayers describe saints, martyrs and archangels triumphing over the dragon who is the incarnation of evil.

The wingless, serpentine Chinese dragon, however, is a sacred, divine creature that represents wisdom, prosperity and good luck. It traditionally symbolizes power, especially control over water, rainfall, typhoons and floods. The dragon and its metaphors are used extensively in Chinese legends, stories, astrology, art, names and idioms.

It normally features the characteristics of nine creatures: a deer's antlers, a camel's head, a demon's eyes, a snake's neck, a clam's belly, a carp's scales, an eagle's claws, a tiger's paws, and a cow's ears.

Fu Xi is a legendary Chinese hero credited with the creation of humanity. He has been described as having the head of a man and the body of a dragon. He is considered one of the first three rulers during the early Chinese dynastic period around 3000 BC. Since then, the Chinese have called themselves "the descendants of the dragon".

The dragon is historically associated with the Emperor of China and used symbolically to represent imperial power. The birth of Liu Bang, founder and first emperor of the Han dynasty

(206 BC–220 AD), was mystical. According to legend, his mother had dreamt of a dragon announcing his birth. During the Sui dynasty (581–618), emperors began to wear dresses with the dragon motif as a symbol of their power. During the Tang dynasty (618–907), high officials were also allowed to wear dragon robes. During the Yuan dynasty (1271–1368), the image of a two-horned and five-clawed dragon was reserved exclusively for the emperor's use, while the image of a four-clawed dragon was used by princes and nobles. As early as the Ming dynasty (1368–1644), the image of a dragon was strictly reserved for the emperor's use. The dragon appeared on the Chinese national flag for the first time during the Qing dynasty (1644–1911). Today, there are stone bas-reliefs of dragons between the stairs of the Forbidden City.

The Chinese astrological zodiac is composed of twelve different animals with their corresponding characteristics. Attracted by the dragon, Chinese families often try to plan pregnancies so that the child is born in the Year of the Dragon, popularly believed to be the year in which leaders and influencers are born. Bruce Lee, also known as "Little Dragon Li", Martin Luther King, Deng Xiaoping and Vladimir Putin were born in the Year of the Dragon.

In the Chinese language, exceptional people are compared to a dragon, while mediocre and unsuccessful people are compared to other despised creatures, such as a worm.

In Chinese symbolism, the mythical phoenix is female and paired with the male dragon; together the two creatures are regarded as a visual metaphor for a balanced, happy and blessed relationship.

The art of conversation

In the Chinese language, there are many expressions or stories advising people to use an implicit means of communication. There is a Chinese saying, "In any meetup, always withhold a third of the words you want to say"—many Chinese consider it to be the golden rule in communicating with others.

This same principle is illustrated in traditional Chinese painting. A technique called "leaving white" is often applied by not filling the surface of the paper. This allows viewers some room for imagination.

There are several reasons why the Chinese prefer to communicate in this way. They have been taught since childhood that if they don't pay attention to what they say, they can suffer a variety of negative consequences in their social relationships. Another Chinese saying warns that "Misfortune comes out of the mouth", so it's not surprising that the Chinese show restraint when speaking.

Another reason is related to Confucian teaching, which advocates seeking out the middle ground in all human endeavors. People believe that in order to achieve success, a balance must be found in all things, including how to communicate with others.

This mode of communication has its origin in many known ancient stories. The Chinese have been inspired by them for thousands of years. Zi Gong, a famous disciple of Confucius, found it extremely regrettable that his master did not accept job offers from various kings. One day, he asked Confucius: "Master, if there is a jade of exceptional beauty, should we sell it or keep it secretly in a cupboard?" Confucius smiled and answered: "If we are offered a good price, let's sell it." Confucius implied that he had not met a good king who shared his values. The Chinese consider this anecdote as the best example of the art of implied conversation.

Zhao Kuangying, the founding emperor of the Song dynasty (950–1127), won power through military revolt. He overthrew the last legitimate emperor of the previous dynasty with the support of a group of warriors. In fear of being overthrown on his return, he organized a banquet to thank these warriors, saying sadly that "If one day someone pushed you to become emperor, like me, you could not refuse". Understanding his fear and innuendoes, the warriors asked to be dismissed and returned to their hometown. The emperor was happy, granting the resignations and compensating them generously with gold and treasure. In addition to its historical value, this story also teaches the Chinese the art of communication through allusion and suggestion.

Non-verbal communication goes much further with the Chinese. Their communication style is indirect, implicit, based on allusion, suggestion, intention, innuendo, or unspoken. It is extremely difficult for Westerners to detect the true intention of Chinese interlocutors, especially in business. Nevertheless, there are some tricks that help to decode the Chinese mind.

The Chinese appreciate it when Western interlocutors make an effort to say a few words in Chinese. Instead of typically repeating "Hello" or "Thank you" in Chinese like everyone else, expressing a few simple phrases to, for example, compliment the city, company, employees, culture or food is highly recommended.

The Chinese inevitably ask "Have you eaten?" or "Have you been out?" These are greetings equivalent to "How are you?" in the West, not to be taken literally or requiring any detailed answer. The correct answer is "Yes" or "Thank you" with a smile.

For Westerners, the word "Yes" suggests agreement or affirmation but for the Chinese it signifies that they are listening. It is a benevolent response showing attention and politeness rather than agreement.

In Chinese custom, negative responses are considered impolite or aggressive. To preserve face is crucial to the

Chinese, so they avoid saying the word "No", preferring instead "I will think about it", "Maybe" or "We'll see". When a Chinese person says, "No big deal" or "The problem is not serious", they often mean that there are still some problems or that the problems may even be serious.

However, the Chinese tend to engage in more direct conversations with insiders. A Chinese person is less reluctant to divulge information with another Chinese. In business, it is common for a Chinese person to speak candidly to an intermediary in an attempt to get the message across to a Westerner who is unfamiliar with Chinese culture. The intermediary may be another Chinese or a Westerner who has spent considerable time in China.

Although the increasing orientation toward market openness and job mobility has contributed to more direct communication in Chinese workplaces, detecting non-verbal clues and understanding communication codes is very useful. The ability to guess and decipher hidden messages is highly desirable. Easily mastering this art of communication is an asset to doing business in China, otherwise the use of an experienced intermediary is advisable.

Topics of conversation

Topics of conversation vary during a meeting between a Westerner and a Chinese. They usually talk about the weather, travel and personal interests. Some topics may elicit more sympathy than others. Choosing a cherished and familiar subject is a good tactic in building a relationship.

In a society marked by a strong spirit of collectivism, traditional Chinese festivals occupy a cardinal place in personal and professional life in China. If Westerners show interest in these festivals and even participate in them, the Chinese could become much more open and friendly towards them.

Proud of the achievements of their ancestors, the Chinese are fond of talking about ancient inventions and telling stories about Zheng He, a heroic explorer during the Ming dynasty. They appreciate it when their Western visitors show interest.

Discussing commonalities often helps to bring people together. The cultural similarities between China and a Western country are topics too often ignored, yet they intrigue the Chinese.

Traditional Chinese Festivals

Traditional Chinese festivals date back to the Shang dynasty (1600–1046 BC) and the Zhou dynasty (1046–256 BC). China has always been a predominantly agricultural country and festivals are essentially part of harvests or prayer offerings, and all follow the Chinese lunar calendar.

Festivals are closely associated with different social customs, each having its own popular activities, ancestral traditions and culinary specialties. Generation after generation, Chinese people celebrate the seven traditional festivals that are part of their cultural heritage and are perfect opportunities for strengthening family, friend and professional ties. Companies use them to thank their employees, customers, partners and local authorities—and to do some advertising.

1. Spring Festival

Spring Festival, also known as Chinese New Year, is celebrated on the first day of the first month of the Chinese lunar calendar year. It is the most important and popular of all Chinese festivals, bringing families together for hearty reunion meals and joyful celebrations. People who have left their homeland must return home. This is why every year, during the twenty-day period surrounding the festival, the transportation network is hectic. During this time, a 500-million-strong human tide pours into train stations, bus stations and airports, producing the largest annual human migration on Earth.

As the spring festival approaches, families thoroughly clean and decorate their homes and people take care of unfinished business and settle outstanding debts (leaving outstanding debts for the new year is considered a bad omen). After affixing Spring Couplets on doors and walls, the whole family gathers to prepare *nian ye fan*, the sumptuous New Year's Eve family reunion dinner that features several auspicious foods, especially the unmissable dumplings.

During the festival, families visit each other, children receive "good luck money" in red envelopes, fireworks are set off, and Mahjong is played. For the past few decades, people all over the country have been meeting on New Year's Eve to watch their favorite TV show on CCTV. The show, called "New Year's Gala", is an entertainment program that lasts almost four hours. China's most celebrated artists offer a grand spectacle of songs, dances, operas, humorous pieces, magic, martial arts and acrobatics. These high-performance productions showcase traditional and modern shows and increasingly include Western artists and celebrities. For example, Canadian singer Céline Dion was the special guest at the 2013 Gala and sang "My Heart Will Go On", and French actress Sophie Marceau was invited in 2014 to sing "La Vie en rose" in a duet with Chinese singer Liu Huan. This is a special occasion for millions of Chinese to watch high-level Western performances.

Chinese New Year celebrations last 15 days until the next festival, the Lantern Festival.

2. Lantern Festival

The Lantern Festival is celebrated on the 15th day of the first month of the Chinese lunar calendar. During this first full moon of the year, locals admire colorful lanterns displayed in the streets, solve riddles hidden in the lanterns, applaud the traditional lion dance, and visit temples to pay homage to the deities. The typical dish accompanying this festival is sticky rice balls filled with sweet red bean paste, sesame paste or peanut butter.

3. Qing Ming Festival

The Qing Ming Festival, also known as "Tomb-Sweeping Day", is the only festival that takes place on a specific date in the international calendar, which could be April 4, 5 or 6 of each year. This is traditionally the time when the temperature rises and the rainy season arrives. In the countryside, the peasants plough and sow.

This festival is not only a seasonal point to guide agricultural work but people also pay their respects to their ancestors or visit the graves of their deceased relatives or friends. On this day there is no cooking; only cold food is served. However, it is not supposed to be a sad festival. Since ancient times and according to tradition, the Chinese enjoy *chun you,* outdoor excursions where families enjoy the pure spring light and children typically fly kites.

4. Duan Wu Festival

The Duan Wu Festival, also known as the Dragon Boat Festival, is celebrated on the fifth day of the fifth month of the Chinese lunar calendar. People enjoy a one-day celebration that includes dragon boat racing.

It has been observed for over 2,000 years to commemorate Qu Yuan, a patriotic poet and politician who lived during the period of the Warring States (475–221 BC) and was a minister under King Huai of Chu. Facing pressure from the powerful Qin state, he made proposals to his king to make his country prosperous and to strengthen the military forces to resist threats. Opposed by the aristocracy, Qu Yuan was removed from office and expelled from the capital. While in exile, he composed several sumptuous poems illustrating his concern for the fate of his home country and his people. His poems became immortal and profoundly influenced Chinese literature. In 278 BC, Qu Yan wrote his last poem, *Huai Sha* ("Regretting the Sand") and committed suicide on the fifth day of the fifth month of the lunar calendar by throwing himself into the Miluo River. According to legend, after Qu Yuan's death, Chu's people flocked to the river bank to pay their last respects to him, and fishermen driving their boats went back and forth on the river hoping to find his body. To prevent him from being eaten by the fish, they threw sticky rice balls into the river.

Since then, the Chinese customarily race dragon boats, eat *zong zi* (sticky rice balls wrapped in reed leaves) and drink rice wine during this festival.

5. Qi Xi Festival

The Qi Xi festival, also known as "Lovers' Day", is celebrated on the seventh day of the seventh month of the Chinese lunar calendar. The festival's origin lies in a beautiful love story passed down the generations.

According to legend, an honest and generous cowherd named Niu Lang (meaning "man who feeds the cow") lived alone raising cattle and cultivating the land. One day, a sky fairy named Zhi Nu (meaning "weaving woman") fell in love with him and secretly came down to earth to marry him. Niu Lang worked in the fields, Zhi Nu wove at home. They had two children and lived a happy life. But their happiness was short-lived. The Queen Mother discovered Zhi Nu's deception and angrily ordered her back to heaven, drawing a permanent barrier with one of her gold hairpins between the husband and wife. An impassable river suddenly appeared in front of Niu Lang. Their mutual fidelity and their sadness touched tens of thousands of magpies who built a bridge by linking their bodies together. The two lovers were then able to meet on the bridge. The Queen Mother finally relented and allowed them to meet there once a year, on the seventh day of the seventh month of the lunar calendar.

Chinese families traditionally gather to commemorate Niu Lang and Zhi Niu and to tell the love story to their children. Nowadays, young people living in urban areas celebrate the feast of Qi xi similarly to Valentine's Day in the West. Flower stores, bars and restaurants are filled with lovers on this day.

6. Mid-Autumn Festival

In the Chinese lunar calendar, the seventh, eighth and ninth months constitute autumn, and the 15th day of the eighth month is celebrated as Mid-Autumn. It is the most important holiday after the Spring Festival. All family members traditionally gather for a family meal when the full moon is at its brightest and roundest. Tasting moon cakes and contemplating the moon are unmissable activities of this celebration. For the Chinese, the roundness of the moon and the moon cakes symbolize reunion and fulfillment.

The festival is closely linked to a children's fairy tale about ten suns that appeared in the sky. The scorching heat dried up the earth and destroyed the crops. People suffered. King Yao order Hou Yi, a talented archer, to shoot down nine of the suns. To thank him, a goddess rewarded him with an immortality potion which his wife Chang-Er accidentally swallowed. She flew to the moon with a jade rabbit as her companion. Later, Hou Yi flew to the sun and, from then on, he and his wife were able to see each other once a month during the full moon. Although a joyful and popular festival, its legend evokes a sense of nostalgia for relatives living far away from the homeland. A Chinese saying is recited on this occasion: "The festival of the moon is the occasion to be homesick and miss loved ones."

7. Chong Yang Festival

The Chong Yang Festival, also known as the Double Ninth Festival, takes place on the ninth day of the ninth month of the Chinese lunar calendar.

In the famous ancient book of divinity *Book of Changes (Yi Jing)*, the number 6 is associated with yin (feminine or negative energy), while the number 9 is associated with yang (masculine or positive energy). Thus, the number 9 in both month and day creates the Chong Yang festival.

To make the most of the yang energy on that day, the Chinese customarily go to a high location in the ancient belief that this strengthens the immune system and repels epidemics. So, people will climb a mountain or tower or go hiking. They also eat traditional Chong Yang cakes and drink chrysanthemum wine.

In 1989, the Chinese government designated the Chong Yang festival as "the festival of the senior citizens" and the younger generations have since adopted the habit of arranging family outings in the countryside aimed at improving the health of the elderly. On this occasion, all central and local government departments organize an autumn outing for retirees.

Four great Chinese inventions

Four great inventions took place in ancient China. Although some modern Chinese historians have argued that other Chinese inventions were perhaps more sophisticated and had a greater impact on Chinese civilization, these four inventions, attributed by Western experts, had a profound impact on the development of civilization throughout the world.

They were originally attributed to Europe, particularly Germany, but Portuguese sailors and Spanish missionaries returning to Europe in the 1530s reported that these inventions had existed in China for centuries.

At the beginning of the 17th century, the English philosopher Francis Bacon, without knowing the origin of these inventions, remarked that they had changed the face of the world and contributed to building the modern West. The idea of the four great Chinese inventions was first proposed by the British sinologist Dr. Joseph Needham (1900–1995) and subsequently accepted by Chinese historians. Today, they are celebrated in China for their historical significance and as symbols of ancient China's advanced science and technology.

1. Compass

During the Warring States period, a device called a *Si Nan* was the precursor of the compass. The *Si Nan* was a ladle-shaped magnet placed on a plate with its handle pointing south. This device evolved over the centuries in China. In the 11th century, tiny magnetized steel needles were invented. Aligned with the earth's magnetic field, one end of a needle pointed north, the other south.

The compass was thus created, greatly improving a ship's ability to navigate long distances. It was introduced in the Arab world and in Europe during the Northern Song dynasty (960–1127). The first mention of a magnetic needle and its use by sailors in Europe can be found in Alexander Neckam's *On the Nature of Things* published in 1190, while the oldest reference to a compass in the Middle East is mentioned in a Persian text dating back to 1232.

2. Papermaking

The invention of paper helped to accelerate the dissemination of knowledge and the development of civilization. Before the appearance of paper, bones, turtle shells and pieces of bamboo were used as writing surfaces. As Chinese civilization developed, they proved to be unsuitable because of their large volume and weight. Hemp fiber and silk were then used to make paper, whose quality was far from satisfactory. Moreover, these two materials were better used for other purposes.

In 105 AD, Cai Lun, a eunuch of the Eastern Han dynasty, invented paper made from fishnet, bark and cloth. These raw materials could be easily found at a much more moderate cost and enabled large-scale paper production.

This papermaking technique was exported to Korea in 384. A Korean monk then brought this know-how to Japan in 610. During a war in the 8th century between the Tang dynasty and the Arab Empire, the Arabs captured Chinese soldiers and papermaking workers. Thus, a paper factory was created by the Arabs. In the 11th century, this know-how was transmitted to India, when Chinese monks went there in search of Buddhist sutras. The first paper mill in Europe was established in Spain around 1150, and in the second half of the 16th century this technology was brought to America. By the 19th century, when paper mills were established in Australia, papermaking had spread worldwide.

Cai Lun is featured in the famous reference book *The 100: A Ranking of the Most Influential Persons in History* by Michael H. Hart. Other personalities featured in this book are Jesus, Buddha, Confucius, Newton, Einstein and Columbus.

3. Printing technique

Inspired by engraved name seals, the Chinese invented the printing of fixed type on a wooden board around 600 AD. This technique played an important role during the Song dynasty, when the empire experienced a phase of education system development. The imperial examinations, or *kējǔ*, encouraged schools to flourish in towns and villages which required a large number of books, treatises and textbooks. The shortcomings of this technique were then revealed. Indeed, it took a long time to complete the engraving of a work. Storing the finished work was difficult and correcting errors was almost impossible.

During the reign of Emperor Song Renzong of the Northern Song dynasty, Bi Sheng invented the printing technique with removable and reusable clay characters which were engraved in porcelain, ceramics or viscous clay and hardened in fire. They were then assembled in resin and wood. This technique revolutionized printing. Due to the large number of different characters in the written Chinese language, this invention had no great impact at the time. In the 12th century, the Korean minister Choe Yun-ui (1102–1162) improved this technique by using metal which was less fragile. Then, the Chinese eunuch Wang Zhen (1290–1333) further modified this technique by using wood, which was less expensive but less accurate than other materials.

The German inventor Johannes Gutenberg was inspired by these results 400 years later when he developed his movable metal type system. Gutenberg's first large-scale printing was a set of 200 illustrated Latin bibles, which came off the presses in 1455. Each copy was pre-sold even before he printed the last page. Gutenberg's printing facility made it possible for the first time to distribute books widely in an efficient and sustainable manner. This actively contributed to the formation of the original information age, the Renaissance.

4. Gunpowder

In Chinese, gunpowder is called *huo yao*, which means "flaming medicine". Unlike papermaking and printing, the birth of gunpowder was quite accidental. It was first invented by alchemists during the Han dynasty when they were trying to make an elixir of immortality. It was a mixture of sulfur, saltpeter, and charcoal. At the end of the Tang dynasty, gunpowder was used for military purposes and for celebrations in the form of fireworks. During the Song and Yuan dynasties, frequent wars stimulated the development of guns and fire arrows launched from bamboo tubes.

According to historical records, gunpowder reached Arab countries, then Greece and other European countries from the 12th or 13th centuries.

Zheng He

To the Chinese, Zheng He (1371–1435) is a hero and a symbol of the advancement of science and technology in ancient China. He was a Chinese Muslim eunuch, sailor, explorer, diplomat and admiral of the Imperial fleet. He lived at the beginning of the Ming dynasty. During the reign of Emperor Zhu Di, also known as Yong Le, Zheng He led seven naval expeditions between 1405 and 1433. His voyages, called "Zheng He to the West" by the Chinese, took him to the south and west of China, through Southeast Asia, South Asia, West Asia and East Africa, to the Persian Gulf and the Red Sea. These were commercial and diplomatic expeditions whose objective was to assert the sovereignty of the Middle Kingdom. By offering Chinese treasures and works of art, Zheng He asked the leaders of the visited countries to recognize the superiority of Chinese culture. In return, they sent their representatives to pay homage to the emperor of China.

Zheng He visited a total of 37 countries and regions and, for each expedition, he had up to 317 ships and 28,000 crew members. The largest ships, carrying hundreds of sailors on four deck levels, were 140 meters long and 50 meters wide.

These extraordinarily costly imperial naval expeditions ceased under the criticism of Emperor Yong Le's successor and his ministers. In order to avoid a revival of the project, the related writings were burned and the ships destroyed, putting an end to Chinese maritime exploration at the time. China then sealed its borders for nearly 500 years.

A British naval officer and former Royal Navy submarine commander, Gavin Menzies, published a book entitled *1421: The Year China Discovered the World*. Following in the footsteps of Zheng He, Menzies spent his life visiting 120 countries, more than 200 museums and libraries and almost every port in the world. He claimed that Zheng He discovered America 70 years before Christopher Columbus, Australia 350 years before Cook, and successfully circumnavigated the globe a century before Magellan.

Menzies theorized that a Venetian map dated 1424 had been signed by Zuane Pizzigano, with precise geographical elements, particularly on Puerto Rico and Guadeloupe, and that Paolo Toscanelli had sent a letter to Christopher Columbus containing a world map initially drawn by the Chinese. Menzies also argued that the first Europeans to arrive in America noted the presence of the Chinese on the continent and that the DNA of the American Indians is closer to that of the Chinese than to

Europeans or Africans. Finally, according to him, many plants observed on the American territory probably came from China.

Cultural similarities

While cultural differences can lead to misunderstandings and difficulties, cultural similarities can bring positive benefits. It is often said that China is very different from the West but few people notice the cultural similarities: Chinese and Americans are pragmatic and efficient in implementing strategies; France and China are famous for their love of the culinary arts; Germans and Chinese share the same sense of discipline and respect for order.

A good example is Switzerland, which was the first Western country to recognize the sovereignty of the PRC in January 1950, three months after China declared its independence. This was 14 years before France, 21 years before the United Nations and 29 years before the United States. As a result, the Chinese people have a sense of gratitude and friendship towards Switzerland. A bilateral free trade agreement was signed between the two countries in 2013 and came into force on July 1, 2014. Switzerland was thus the first Western country to conclude such an agreement with China. Seven cultural similarities between the Chinese and the Swiss may have contributed to this agreement:

1. Color red

The Chinese attach great importance to the color red. In Switzerland, red is also omnipresent, notably on the flag, the passport and the uniforms of the national sports teams, which, from the Chinese point of view, creates a natural affinity between the two countries.

2. Artistic expression

Artistic expression reflects a sensitivity, a preference and a culture. Paper cutting is a typical Chinese craft. It dates back to the 6th century, when women glued gold and silver rods to their hair at the temples and men used them in sacred rituals. Paper cutting was later used at festivals and weddings to decorate doors and windows. After hundreds of years of development, it has become a very popular means of decoration in China.

Although paper cutting originated in Asia and spread throughout Central Europe in the 17th century, devotional images and heraldic paper cuts made by nuns were among the first paper cutting in Switzerland. In the second half of the 18th century, silhouette portraits became fashionable in Swiss cities as a cheaper alternative to oil miniatures. Johann Wolfgang von Goethe, Jean Huber and Johann Caspar Lavater made them popular. Paper cuts in different shapes were then used to illustrate stories. They became popular in rural areas, with Johann Jakob Hauswirth and Louis Saugy being among the greatest rural paper cutters. Today, one can visit a paper cutting museum at the Château d'Oex in Switzerland.

3. Humility

Humility is one of the three treasures of Taoism, the guiding philosophy of Chinese culture. Chinese children are taught never to brag. A Chinese proverb holds that "It is the bird in front of the fight that gets shot first". According to another, "The tallest tree attracts strong winds". This sage advice discourages the Chinese from being haughty and pretentious.

Modesty is a common rule in the Chinese socialization process. When someone receives a compliment, they automatically respond with the expression *na li na li*, which literally means "Where? Where?" and is used to deflect praise. In Chinese culture, openly accepting a compliment is considered rude.

In Chinese language, flattering titles or words are always reserved for others and those of lesser value are used to describe oneself. This can go as far as exaggeration. This phenomenon is often misunderstood by Westerners, who might think that the Chinese lack self-confidence.

As the world's largest market and the world's second-largest economy, China insists in the media and at all international conferences and meetings that it is a developing country and wants other countries to see it that way.

Switzerland is one of the richest countries in the world. In the 2019 rankings for (nominal) GDP per capita, it was ranked third after Luxembourg and the Macao SAR and projected IMF estimates as of April 2021 put the top three as Luxembourg, Switzerland and Ireland. Nevertheless, Swiss people tend to have a simple and natural lifestyle and many travel by bicycle or use public transport. The bus and train networks are among the most developed in the world.

The Swiss appreciate nature, spending their weekends and vacations in the mountains or near a lake, and enjoying activities such as hiking and sailing. The quintessential Swiss chalets are simple structures in harmony with nature and in the continuity of tradition. The Swiss love their traditional foods, especially veal sausages, raclette and fondue. This typical Swiss cuisine can be considered rustic in the eyes of many in other countries.

The Swiss believe in "small is beautiful", which describes their national spirit. Despite the worldwide success of Swiss multinationals such as Nestlé, Novartis, UBS and ABB, 99% of Swiss companies are SMEs (small and medium-sized enterprises) with less than 250 employees. It is a political will to preserve the region's know-how and develop the local economic fabric.

Swiss people are generally reserved and humble. Although Switzerland is a country of banks, Swiss bankers are discreet and advocate modesty. This is part of the heritage of the Protestant religion and Calvinism.

4. Hard-working

Wherever they are, Overseas Chinese always quickly gain a reputation for being hard-working. Their children work more than others at school and Chinese restaurants and stores are usually the only ones that remain open for long hours and often seven days a week. Chinese employees are more willing to work evenings and weekends.

In China, primary and secondary school students spend an average of three hours a day on homework, double the world average. They study 77 hours a week.

China has adopted the 9-9-6 working system, i.e., employees work from 9:00 a.m. to 9:00 p.m., six days a week. In recent years, some high-tech companies have even used this system as an official work schedule. Jack Ma, the founder of Alibaba, was noted for his comments praising his company's 9-9-6 work culture: "Being able to work in 9-9-6 is a great joy...If you want to join Alibaba, you must be prepared to work 12 hours a day."

Under Western influence, Chinese companies are beginning to offer wellness programs to their employees, including financial support for gym memberships, the provision of meditation or yoga rooms in shared workspaces, or sponsored vacations. For the time being, these programs do not appear to have been successful with Chinese employees. Being happy at work, which means maintaining good relations with colleagues and superiors, is most important to them, which translates into spending long hours at work with co-workers.

But there has been a trend in the opposite direction. For example, executives of various Suzhou-based international companies reported that after implementing more benefits and flexibility in the workplace for their employees, they have noticed increasing laziness and a refusal to work overtime.

Figures show that in general the more prosperity increases, the more working hours decrease. But there are a few exceptions, notably Singapore and Hong Kong where the majority of the population is of Chinese origin. Despite their high economic wealth, Singaporeans and Hong Kongers continue to work as much as the Chinese in mainland China.

Switzerland likes to portray itself as a country of hard workers. It certainly does have an international image of being punctual and meticulous but, compared to the rest of the world, the Swiss are not especially hard-working. Nevertheless, in an international comparison report published in 2020 by Eurostat, Swiss employees were described as the most hard-working in Europe, followed by Icelanders, who work an average of 42 hours per week.

In 2002, Swiss voters rejected a proposal to reduce the working week from 42 to 36 hours and, in 2012, they rejected another proposal to increase the minimum annual paid vacation for employees from four weeks to six weeks.

5. Frugality

Frugality is a central value of Taoism. The Chinese are proud of their tradition of diligence and thrift and their principle of "honor to frugality and shame to extravagance". One of the most-loved ancient Chinese emperors was Guang Wudi (141– 87 BC), a caring and generous man who emphasized culture and listened to the people's difficulties. Known for his frugality and moderation, he advocated thrift and knew how to reward virtuous people. Chinese historians have labeled him as the "most humane" emperor of all the dynasties.

The Chinese government regularly takes action against hedonism and excessive spending in public institutions, such as state-owned enterprises, financial institutions, and district and municipal governments. For example, in order to enforce the rules of frugality, inspectors of the disciplinary control body reveal violations on the organization of expensive dinners. Those using government cars or office space for personal use are sanctioned. The people are encouraged to report violators to the authorities.

In the summer of 2020, President Xi Jinping stressed the importance of resolutely ending food waste in the country and called for the promotion of frugality. Calling the issue of food waste shocking and distressing, Xi stressed the need to maintain a sense of crisis in food policy, especially in the face of the fallout from the Covid-19 epidemic, despite the fact that China has recorded consecutive bumper harvests in recent years.

According to figures published by the World Bank, China's national savings rate was 51% in 2007 and 47% in 2017. China's economic growth has slowed somewhat in recent years, but these savings rate figures are still some of the most impressive in the world.

Banking activities in Switzerland began at the beginning of the 15th century through wholesale trade. Over the centuries, banking has developed into a complex, regulated and international industry. The preservation of the wealth of the rich from all over the world has become a national culture and tradition.

In spite of their high income, the Swiss have a tradition of reusing second-hand goods through a system of barter sales. Every spring, the population participates in a fair where everyone can sell used clothes or goods at low prices. Swiss children are used to having a piggy bank from a young age.

For decades, Switzerland has had one of the world's highest national savings rates. According to the World Bank, this rate was 34% in 2017, putting the country in 10th position out of 170 countries, one of the highest among European countries.

6. Cultural diversity

China wins the Golden Palm when it comes to cultural diversity. It has 56 ethnic groups, plus 300 languages and dialects, and all the world's major religions. The Han ethnic group accounts for 92% of the population. The other ethnic groups are traditionally called "minorities" (*shao shu min zu*). Each ethnic group has its own language. Within the Han ethnic group, each province has its own dialect; each dialect varies from one city to another, and from one village to another. According to a United Nations report, China has had no migrants from other parts of the world for centuries, which is mainly due to cultural barriers, including language.

The Chinese state encourages the rise of ethnic expression as long as it does not lead to separatism. China is proudly multicultural. Themes relating to minority cultures occupy a prominent place in contemporary Chinese painting and graphic design. Television stations broadcast daily programs about these cultures and their history, art and customs. Books about these cultures find a large market in China. Tourism in minority regions has become a favorite activity of the Han Chinese. Chinese banknotes are printed in five languages: Mandarin, Mongolian, Tibetan, Uygur and Zhuang.

China has no official religion as no common religion was originated in China. While many Chinese citizens practice no religion, others belong to one of the four recognized religions: Christianity, Buddhism, Islamism and Judaism.

Cultural diversity exists and has been respected in Switzerland since its foundation. Article 2.2 of the current Swiss Constitution, most of which dates back to the founding of the Swiss Confederation in 1848, states that the Swiss Confederation "shall promote the common welfare, sustainable development, internal cohesion and cultural diversity of the country".

Immigration flows to Switzerland from the 15th century onwards varied. Switzerland at different times proved to be a welcoming land for foreigners, lying at the crossroads of several European cultures. Today, with a population of around eight million, Switzerland has four official languages: German, French, Italian and Romansh. Switzerland's organization is a true example of multiculturalism within a single nation in Europe.

Switzerland has experienced widespread immigration over the last two decades. According to the latest figures, the percentage of immigrants in Switzerland is around 25%. More than 80% of foreigners living in Switzerland come from European countries. Nationals from Germany, Italy, Portugal and France alone make up almost half of the foreigners residing in Switzerland. The populations from Asia, Africa and America are approximately 170,000, 110,000 and 80,000, respectively. This adds an element of international multiculturalism to the intrinsic multicultural configuration of Switzerland. (63)

Another determining factor in Swiss culture is religion. Most people living in Switzerland are Christian, with about 35.8% Roman Catholics and 23.8% Protestants. But many other religions are also represented in Switzerland: 5.3% Muslims, 0.5% Buddhists and 0.2% Jews. The percentage of people who do not belong to any religion is 26.3%. (64)

7. Peace and Neutrality

In pursuing comprehensive friendly relations and cooperation with other countries, China's foreign policy is based on *li shang wang lai*—obligation and reciprocity. China believes that nations should treat each other with courtesy and respect, and resolutely opposes interference in the internal affairs of another nation. While it has fought numerous wars to protect its borders and secure peace for its people, at no point in its millennia-long history has China ever sent military troops into a foreign country with a view to occupying it. The Chinese are peace-loving and, despite their growing political, economic and military power, they have no interest in posing a threat to international peace and security.

Neutrality is one of Switzerland's main foreign policy principles: the country shall not get involved in armed or political conflicts between other states. This policy is self-imposed, permanent and armed, designed to ensure external security and promote peace. Switzerland has not participated in a foreign war since its neutrality was established by the Treaty of Paris in 1815 and did not join the United Nations until 2002. Nevertheless, it pursues an active foreign policy and is frequently involved in peace-building processes around the world.

Business meetings

Etiquette and protocol have become indispensable standards for all business meetings in the West. Knowing and applying the principles of etiquette also shows the consideration that one has for one's partners. Lack of etiquette and poor planning are the two main reasons why many business meetings fail. We don't get a second chance to make a good first impression. This rule also applies to Chinese business meetings which are generally conducted like those in the West but are more ritualized.

When planning a meeting with Chinese partners, special attention should be paid to holiday closings. Apart from traditional Chinese festivals, May 1st, October 1st and the week thereafter should be avoided because the whole country is on vacation and organizing meetings with key people will prove very difficult.

Punctuality is paramount. Being late for a meeting is a serious gaffe in Chinese corporate culture and is considered disrespectful. If something unexpected occurs, Chinese partners should be informed as soon as possible.

Chinese businessmen expect their interlocutors to be well prepared for the meeting. For example, relevant documents should be printed in sufficient quantities and ready for distribution. The presentation should be first class, a sign of respect for the participants. The agenda should be sent to each participant at least one week in advance and should include the start and end times.

The host company should specify the dress code in advance. In general, suits and ties are standard for employees of companies in large Chinese cities, especially during meetings with Westerners. In the Tier-3 and Tier-4 Chinese cities, formal dress is often not required.

In China, people usually enter the meeting room in hierarchical order. The first person to enter is thus considered the head of the delegation.

Table seating is defined according to rank, such as hierarchical importance and seniority. The central seat facing the door is the most important and is customarily occupied by the chairperson. There are fixed seating places for hosts and guests. In general, guests are seated on the left side of the chairperson, participants of the host group on the right, because the Chinese tradition considers the left side more noble and honorable than the right.

It is customary to have small informal discussions before the meeting begins. They serve to relax the atmosphere and put the participants at ease. The topics of conversation mentioned above can be raised in these discussions.

The Chinese are not shy to talk about the details of their private life, such as their age, origin, marital status or even their salary. Older people are more likely to ask their interlocutor questions related to their private life. This is a sign of attention. Younger people are more discreet towards their Western interlocutors out of respect for their culture.

It is not uncommon for Chinese hosts to ask questions that may surprise their Western guests. The perception of privacy differs significantly between Chinese and Western cultures. Westerners attach great importance to individualism and privacy, hence their inclination to protect personal information. Chinese society advocates collectivism and sharing within the community. The notion of *yin si* ("concealment of the secret") is largely negative in Chinese culture.

Meetings with the Chinese can follow a fairly formal structure, especially with government entities. The leading member of the host party introduces themself and their colleagues, and then presents their views on the purpose of the meeting. The leading member of the guests should then do the same. Subordinate members of the Chinese delegation generally do not speak unless requested to do so by the leading member. Guests are expected to follow the same protocol.

Restraint, calm and good emotional control during the meeting are appreciated and recommended. Silence is considered a sign of respect and caution. Not asking too many questions helps to save face for oneself, for the other person and for the group. Using kind words, being polite, and smiling lightly is appreciated behavior.

Once the initial meeting is over, gifts are often offered to the guests. In some cases, gifts are exchanged between the two parties. When a visit to the host company is planned, a group photograph is always taken at the end of the visit as a souvenir. If the meeting takes place in a neutral location, guests customarily leave before the hosts.

Business meals

Meals in China are part of the important process of developing business relationships. A relationship of trust leading to open and clear exchanges is the key to success in all cultures. In China, such relationships are personal. For the Chinese, business relationships must be amicable, and Chinese businessmen and women seek above all to make friends before committing to doing business together because friendship generates trust, loyalty and favors.

Building a business relationship in China is primarily done through entertainment activities such as business meals. These are unique opportunities to create networks and friendships. The business meal is a casual moment often followed by a karaoke outing where everyone can relax and be spontaneous and joyful. After the meal, traditional massage sessions are often offered.

Business meals are numerous and frequent in China. They are known to be copious, long and full of customs and traditions. As with meetings, the Chinese usually enter the dining room in hierarchical order. Seniority is equally respected so that elders, even of lower rank, are often invited to enter first. Respect for elders is observed in all Chinese social activities, and the entourage will often notice and criticize a lack of respect.

Seating is dictated by hierarchy or seniority. Those who are hierarchically superior or more senior sit in the center, facing the entrance. Guests should wait for their seats to be designated. They are usually invited to sit next to the head of the host company. Chiefs and senior staff sit before others.

During a business meal in China, repeated toasts while sending each other good wishes is standard procedure. People send each other all kinds of compliments to show admiration, respect and friendship. The hosts always put food on the guests' plates as a sign of hospitality.

During a business meal, up to 20 or 30 dishes can be served. The trick is to taste only a little of each dish. An empty plate traditionally means that the person is always hungry. Guests therefore continue to offer them food. Leaving a little food on the plate signals that the person has eaten enough. As a result of the new Chinese policy against food waste, it is now advisable not to over-order but rather to clear the plates. Nevertheless, during a Chinese business meal, many specialties are expected to be served.

Tipping is not a Chinese custom and can be considered contemptuous since it may imply that the servers are short of money.

In a commercial context, it is usually the person who invites that ends up paying the bill. But do so discreetly by going directly to the cashier without being noticed by the others.

Culture of hard liquor consumption

One of the most peculiar traditions at Chinese business meals is the culture of drinking strong alcohol. Participants constantly invite each other to fill and empty their glasses. To refuse is to make the other person lose face—an unwise move. Though many Chinese roundly disapprove of this practice, it has been going on for thousands of years in China. Advocates believe that it helps to set a joyful atmosphere and bring people together. Some even use it to test the ability of their interlocutors to handle hard liquor. The drink of choice is the powerful baijiu, a whisky usually distilled from cereals, sorghum or, more rarely, sticky rice. It can be mixed with corn, wheat, barley from Tibet, or millet. The alcohol content can reach 70%.

This culture of hard liquor drinking could date back to 2000 BC. According to a story told from generation to generation, a prince named Du Kang invented this drink. He had been sent by his father to guard the food warehouse. He was called one day to examine the damage caused by a heavy storm. Having seen drops falling from the roof, he tasted them and found them good. It was actually rain mixed with fermented grain. However, there was a hint of earth. He thought about it and tried unsuccessfully for a long time to eliminate this taste. One night he dreamed of a god who passed on the secret of the recipe to him. He was asked to randomly choose three people the next day at around 7 p.m. and added drops of their blood to the drink. He eventually selected an intellectual, a warrior and an idiot. Baijiu is therefore reputed to have these three characters that represent the three states of the human mind. Since then, the Chinese have used strong alcohol to decipher the character and potential of their interlocutors.

One type of baijiu is called Maotai. Welcoming your guests with it is a sign of privilege in China. This liquor distilled from fermented sorghum, Maotai is produced in the town of Maotai in Guizhou province. Its fame dates back to the Qing dynasty when northern Chinese distillers introduced a more advanced technique to the south to create a distinct type of baijiu. During the Civil War at the beginning of the 20th century, the Chinese People's Liberation Army camped at Maotai and took part in the sale of local alcohol. This commercial activity enabled the army to finance the fight. Following the Communist victory in the war, the Chinese government grouped the local distilleries into a state-owned enterprise called Guizhou Maotai. From then on, Maotai became an indispensable prestige drink at state banquets.

Today, Maotai contains 53% alcohol, is sold only on the Chinese market, and is one of the world's best-selling drinks. Listed only on the Chinese stock exchange, its market value exceeds that of giants such as Coca-Cola, Toyota, Nike and Disney.

Chinese cuisine

Chinese gastronomy has gradually been formed in the development of the society. It has helped to shape the character and temperament of the Chinese people. In the panorama of Chinese culture, cuisine is generally considered as one of the best ways to get to know China.

Its culinary culture is based on a deep philosophy. Eating and drinking are particularly important to the Chinese, not only for their physical well-being but also for their mental health and overall harmony. This may seem strange to Westerners, so it's worth looking at in some detail.

Chinese cuisine is closely related to traditional Chinese medicine. The yin-yang concept is also applied in the kitchen. In traditional medicine, yin represents everything that is feminine, slow, silent, descending, internal and stable, such as a woman, her internal organs, abdomen and lower part of her body. Yang represents everything that is masculine, fast, active, ascending, external and energetic, such as a man, the surface of his body, limbs and upper part of his body. The vital processes of the human body are manifestations of the movement of yin-yang energy. When balanced, they complement and reinforce each other, and the body enjoys good health. When unbalanced, it causes disharmony, the body functions improperly, and good health is impacted.

In the West, a typical balanced diet includes carbohydrates, protein, fat, fiber, vitamins and minerals. In China, people believe in balancing the yin and yang of the body, which can be achieved by eating the right foods and taking into account their properties, cooking methods, flavors, and personal and climatic factors.

The Chinese traditionally believe that food has yin or yang characteristics, i.e., warming or cooling properties. Warming foods are meat, garlic, pepper, ginger, sugar, wine, apricots and black tea. They are often spicy, with a high caloric content, and are believed to have stimulating functions. Cooling foods are often low in calories and pale in color, such as celery, cucumber, crab, freshwater clams, persimmons and green tea.

These are good in hot weather or when there is excessive internal heat in the body, which traditional Chinese medicine considers a cause of illness.

Chinese cuisine features an array of cooking methods but the most common are stir-frying, deep-frying, shallow-frying, roasting, braising, boiling and steaming. Frying and roasting are considered yang, whereas boiling and steaming are yin.

According to traditional Chinese medicine, different flavors are associated with different organs of the body. Acid is associated with the liver, sweet with the spleen, bitter with the heart, spicy with the lungs, and salty with the kidneys. According to a traditional belief, the organs of some animals are beneficial for the same organs of humans. This is why eating offal has always been popular. The Chinese also believe that certain food can have a beneficial effect in curing a disease. For example, soy curd treats arteriosclerosis, dried mushrooms treat high blood pressure, red beans treat anemia, and pears treat cough.

The uniqueness of Chinese cuisine lies not only in its philosophy, presentation, flavor, cooking techniques and aromas, but also in its numerous styles of preparation. China traditionally has more than 60 cooking styles, eight of which are very well known. They have developed in response to the diversity of resources and climate in each region. During a business meal, a Westerner is often offered one of the following four styles, which are Chinese favorites:

1. Huaiyang cuisine

Huaiyang is a region in eastern China, geographically located between the south and north. As a result, Huaiyang's cuisine has been influenced by different styles of cuisine in the country.

Due to its warm climate and fertile soil, this region produces many types of vegetables and rice. Although each town has its own specialties, this cuisine commonly emphasizes the freshness and original flavor of the raw material. It uses mushrooms, fish, vegetables and tofu as the main ingredients and is known for its sweetness.

Delicacy is a distinctive feature of this cuisine. The local people want to transform the ingredients in an exquisite way. Portions are usually small and refined and are meticulously prepared by the expert chef who needs intricate knife skills.

Some of the best dishes are those prepared with seafood, especially fish, eel, turtles and local crabs. Stews prepared using the red cooking method are popular—food is gently cooked with broth and soy sauce. Sticky rice cakes are also a local specialty.

2. Guangdong cuisine

Guangdong or Cantonese cuisine, called Yue in Chinese, is very popular throughout China. Guangdong, located in southern China, is a subtropical coastal region with a favorable climate for producing an abundant selection of fruits, vegetables, herbs, seafood and meat. Guangdong cuisine is characterized by delicacy, lightness and a wide range of ingredients.

The Cantonese have retained many ancient eating customs. Everything that walks, crawls, flies or swims is edible. Although some foods may seem strange to Chinese from other regions and to foreigners, Cantonese dishes are generally very tasty. The most popular Cantonese dishes are sweet and sour pork, cold ground chicken, gold-roasted suckling pig and stewed chicken, as well as delicious slow-cooked soups. Stir-frying, roasting and steaming are the most common cooking methods. Vegetables are lightly cooked to keep them crunchy. There are many ways to cook seafood. One is steaming. The best-known dish cooked in this way is steaming fresh fish to which small pieces of fresh ginger and green onions are added. This dish is served with a special sauce, secretly prepared by each chef.

Dim sum, which has in recent years become increasingly popular in Western countries, is typical of Cantonese cuisine, comprising bite-sized dumplings, steamed buns, pancakes stuffed with rice dough, meatballs, egg rolls and small portions of soup. Cantonese cuisine is well known in the West, especially in the United States since the Cantonese imported it when they came to North America as gold diggers and railway builders in the 19th century.

3. Northern cuisine

Northern cuisine in Chinese is a general term used to describe various styles of cooking in northern China. Among them, the Beijing style is the most famous for its imperial cuisine.

Northern cuisine primarily relies on meaty and starchy foods and liberally uses garlic and green onions. It is a robust cuisine in which food is usually prepared more simply than in the south. Slow-cooked, braised and simmered dishes are characteristic of northern food. Some vegetables, such as cabbage, are marinated to be preserved during the long cold winter.

Geographically close to Mongolia, Northern cuisine is influenced by Muslim and Mongolian tastes and is famous for its mutton and lamb-based dishes, especially lamb sautéed with shallots.

Wheat is the staple crop in this region, with many dishes made from wheat flour. Specialties include dumplings, stuffed buns, pancakes and many styles of noodles.

Although Beijing's cuisine is classified as a subdivision of Northern cuisine, the city has developed its own style of cuisine by absorbing the best features of the country's different regional styles. Beijing cuisine, which is based on the Tang family-style cuisine, originated in the imperial kitchens of the Qing dynasty and features three main characteristics. First, the dishes are both sweet and savory, incorporating both northern and southern styles. According to a Chinese saying, southerners have a sweet tooth while northerners are thirsty for salt. Beijing dishes manage to satisfy both. Second, the dishes are generally well cooked and strongly flavored. The elderly particularly enjoy these well-salted dishes. Third, this type of cooking pays special attention to the natural flavors of the ingredients, so seasonings are rarely used.

Peking lacquered duck is a world-renowned Chinese dish that was exclusively reserved for imperial cuisine during the Qing dynasty. Legend has it that ducks were raised by eating rice and smelling the spring scent of the Xiang Mountain, located in the west of Beijing. Xiang means "perfume" and imperial chefs roasted these ducks over a fire of peach and pear woods. This technique was adopted by cooks all over Beijing before gaining nationwide popularity.

4. Sichuan cuisine

Located in a mountainous region in southwest China, Sichuan has a year-round humid climate. According to traditional Chinese medicine, moisture that stays in our bodies for a long time is detrimental to our health. The inhabitants of this region like to drive moisture out of their bodies by eating fiery and spicy foods. Chilies, local pepper, garlic and ginger are essential ingredients in Sichuan cuisine.

Several specialties are known in China and abroad. Mapo tofu consists of minced pork, tofu, chili peppers and Sichuan pepper. Gong Bao chicken is made with chicken cubes sautéed with chili peppers, peanuts or mahogany. Other popular dishes are twice-cooked pork, spicy crispy fish, spicy Chongqing hotpot, steamed pork with rice flour, sliced marinated beef, beef tongue with spicy sauce, and flavored noodles.

Symbolism of chopsticks

Chopsticks occupy a unique place in Chinese culture. Much more than just tableware, chopsticks are considered to be auspicious objects and are indispensable at weddings and other important social events. In pairs, they represent the yin-yang duality, with round and square sides symbolizing the Taoist concept of "round sky and square earth". They are stronger and longer than Japanese and Korean chopsticks. Japanese chopsticks are usually pointed; Korean chopsticks are flatter.

The Chinese revere chopsticks as mythical and divine. Recorded history traces their origin back 3,000 years and there are three main legends about their invention. One is that Da Yu (2100 BC), a legendary king and hero known for combatting incessant flooding, converted tree branches into chopsticks to save time when eating hot food. Another relates that a concubine of the last emperor of the Shang dynasty invented jade chopsticks to please her emperor. Yet another tells of Jiang Ziya, a noble and minister of the first king of the Zhou dynasty, who made the first bamboo chopsticks based on the advice of a divine bird.

Chopsticks are noble objects for the Chinese. Many historical writings confirm that they were first used by emperors, kings and aristocrats in ancient China. Later, they were also used in cults and spiritual ceremonies.

There are several taboos surrounding the use of chopsticks. Don't cross them over each other: this is a sign of denial of others at the table. Don't place them vertically in a bowl: this is reserved for funerals. Don't point them at others. And don't tap them on tableware: this is associated with begging.

Business negotiations

Negotiation is an inevitable and decisive step in business. For Western businessmen, this task is especially difficult in China. Cultural differences complicate all aspects of the process which involves customs, beliefs and tactics. Whereas Westerners negotiate with the aim of concluding a business contract, the Chinese negotiate to establish a new friendly relationship through which they can do business with trust.

Business negotiations in China take time. Before engaging in them, the Chinese want to make sure that their partners are worthy. They spend a lot of energy on recreational activities with their potential partners, and a lot of time on sharing business meals, shopping and sightseeing. During this time, they closely observe their potential partners and watch for things that might jeopardize their future business relationship.

As the Chinese attach great importance to ritual, commercial negotiation is no exception. Before starting the process, they take care to remind each other about the essential values of tradition, namely the importance of respect, sincerity and tolerance. Proverbs, sayings and stories are exchanged to create a friendly atmosphere. Finally, they generally end by quoting the following popular saying: "Friendship first, business second. If the business fails, friendship remains." This resembles a warning before a match.

In a society strongly influenced by hierarchy, negotiations must always be initiated and carried out between people at the same hierarchical level. The opposite would be perceived as disrespectful and unacceptable.

According to a Chinese saying, "Business is a battlefield". Many Chinese negotiating tactics are found in ancient books, most famously Sun Zi's *The Art of War*. Some of the following tactics are commonly practiced.

"Fatigue" tactics are intended to make negotiations last longer. Chinese businessmen can delay negotiations by showing that they are not interested. Keeping long silence is also a common tactic. They may also say that they need time to think or to talk to someone with more decision-making power.

They may knowingly extend negotiations well beyond the agreed time frame.

Being frugal, the Chinese practice bargaining to get a better price. However, they are willing to make the effort and give in on many other aspects if their request, for example on price, is met by their negotiating partners. The Chinese believe in compromise; for them, the concept of "win-win" is Western.

The tactic known as "make noise in the east, attack in the west" is a diversionary tactic. This allows Chinese negotiators to make concessions in areas that they claim are important, and in return they demand compensation only in the area that is really important to them.

Surprise tactics often have a decisive impact on negotiations. As they approach the end of the negotiation, the Chinese may suddenly announce a change of agenda. This may be the time, place, team, or person in charge of the negotiation. The goal is to create a small disruptive element in order to gain some advantages.

Historically, the first encounter between the Western world and China was brutal and resulted in The Century of Humiliation which is a deep vein of injustice that the Chinese still feel today following their subjugation by Western powers between 1840 and 1949, notably their defeats in the two Opium Wars and the Eight-Power Allied War of Aggression. The latter conflict was against the Qing dynasty, led by the British Empire, the United States, France, Germany, Russia, Japan, Austria, and Italy. These three wars were initiated by Western countries in the 19th and 20th centuries. Some Chinese negotiators use the historical fact of the "Century of Humiliation" as a guilt tactic in hopes of obtaining concessions from their Western partners.

Due to holistic thinking, the Chinese tend to consider all terms simultaneously in the negotiation process. The negotiating agenda is only a starting point for discussions; many points can be added later. The Chinese think in a circular mode while Westerners think in a linear mode.

The Chinese like to use the support of an intermediary in a commercial negotiation. The intermediary is often someone who knows both parties well. This increases the level of trust. The intermediary can facilitate communication by managing difficult issues. In the event of an impasse, the intermediary can help to resolve a difficult situation by offering concessions to each party. This can often turn the situation around completely and achieve success. For Western companies, the use of an intermediary often pays off. For example, the Chinese appreciate it when they learn that the intermediary is a friend or partner of the negotiator, regardless of whether the intermediary is a Chinese or a foreigner long resident in China, because it shows a commitment to the country.

Concerning the Chinese decision-making process in a negotiation, several phenomena deserve special attention.

Decisions are generally made by the highest-ranking Chinese managers but the group culture remains paramount.

Sometimes a large Chinese negotiating team is present in the meeting room. Only the most senior member speaks while the rest of the team gathers information. The real decision is not made immediately but is made in internal meetings between negotiation sessions.

Chinese governmental entities are slower in making decisions than Chinese private companies. This is due to their complex structure and traditional working style. When negotiating with large Chinese companies, whether private or state-owned, the heads of different hierarchies and departments appear in the negotiation. The appearance of a mid-level manager from the commercial or technical department to review aspects of business implementation usually signals the end is near and the negotiation successful.

The Chinese rarely criticize at the negotiating table. Once the negotiations are over, Western negotiators may mistakenly believe that agreement has been reached. They could then feel frustrated and confused when they realize that it is not. Chinese partners may make a sudden and unexpected request, for example to amend the contract on a point that has already been discussed and agreed upon. It is also possible that the Chinese do not communicate their willingness to make a change but present a contract containing different terms and conditions from those agreed upon in previous discussions. For them, this is not considered a breach of contract. What they see is a constantly changing world where adaptability is a universal quality for a long-term partnership.

The concept of a contract is relatively new in China. One's word has always been enough, as evidenced from a well-known Confucian quote: "The word of a virtuous man will not be caught by a horse." The Chinese generally do not engage a lawyer at the beginning of a negotiation. If a lawyer is present at the meeting, it may be a sign that the negotiation is nearing completion.

The success of a commercial negotiation in China is always crowned by a solemn signing ceremony. The smooth running of such a ceremony brings luck to the future cooperation of the parties. The date and place of the ceremony are carefully chosen. Chinese companies do not hesitate to hire professionals in feng shui, the Chinese divinatory philosophy that aims to harness energy forces and establish harmony between an individual and their environment.

On the day of signing, all participants in the negotiations must be present. They enter the premises together, greet each other, shake hands and sit down. At the time of signing, members of both parties position themselves behind their respective representatives. After the signing, both representatives stand up at the same time, exchange texts and shake hands to congratulate each other on their fruitful cooperation. Then, all participants express their joy and congratulations with warm applause and a souvenir group photo is taken.

The impact of Confucianism in business

During his official visit to China in 2018, French President Emmanuel Macron spent three days with Chinese President Xi Jinping and other senior Chinese politicians. Before departing for Beijing International Airport, he suddenly asked for a private visit, without journalists, to the Temple of Confucius. He explained later that he realized that, to understand China, one must understand Confucius and Confucianism.

Though China is a vast country of different ethnicities, cultures and geographical regions, its ideology is largely homogeneous and deeply influenced by the classical teachings of Confucianism, a philosophy in search of unity and harmony in a society of diversity.

Confucius

Understanding the context of the historical period in which Confucius lived is essential to appreciating him and the development of Confucianism. After the Shang dynasty, the Zhou dynasty's vast territory was divided. The Zhou king had direct control over only a small part of the kingdom; he received symbolic tributes from the feudal states. Yet the Zhou dynasty lasted longer than any other dynasty in Chinese history (almost 800 years). The first half was the Western Zhou (1046–771 BC), the second half the Eastern Zhou (770–256 BC), which was divided into two periods: Spring and Autumn, and Warring States. It marked the transition from tribal to feudal society in ancient China.

The Western Zhou period is known to have been geopolitically quite peaceful. The society lived mainly on agriculture and animal husbandry. The land was drawn into square plots divided into nine equal parts. Eight peasant families shared the eight outer plots and combined their efforts and resources to cultivate the central plot, whose harvest was destined for the nobility. The nobles, who owned an army, ensured social security and order. Succeeding Chinese dynasties considered this system the fairest way of distributing arable land.

From 770 BC, the king of Zhou gradually lost his authority and the feudal states revolted to gain independence or take over power. Wars between and within the states were frequent. The people suffered and the leaders were anxious. During this tormented period, in spite of these perpetual fights, the culture continued to develop. Chinese philosophy reached its zenith. Many schools of thought emerged, giving rise to the phenomenon known as the Contention of a Hundred Schools of Thought that saw the birth of China's greatest thinkers, including Lao Zi (Taoism) and Confucius (Confucianism). Their philosophical influence has endured for 2,500 years and continues to influence Chinese culture and social consciousness.

Confucius (551–479 BC) was born in Zou county, Lu State, now Shandong province. He was a teacher, politician and philosopher. According to historical sources, his upbringing was difficult. He lost his father at the age of three and his mother at the age of 17. This left him no choice but to study to find a way to earn a living later. Thanks to his precocious taste for books and rituals, he was able to become a tutor at the age of 17. He understood the importance of education and by the age of 20 he had his first disciples. Famous by the age of 30, his eventful political career really took off when he reached 50 but it was short-lived, lasting only four years before he was forced to resign when he was unable to reach agreement with the leader of the Lu kingdom and its ministers. He then traveled throughout the kingdom and its states for 14 years until, at the age of 68, he returned to his native Lu. Rejecting all offers for a political position, he devoted himself to teaching, remaining a respected gentleman with no government responsibilities until his death at the age of 73.

Although Confucius worked in government positions, he gained an honorable reputation through his teachings. Deeply concerned with education, his quotes became part of the daily Chinese fabric. Two illustrate the importance of study: "If I walk among a trio, one of the two companions is surely my teacher" and "Studying without thinking leads to confusion, and thinking without studying leads to laziness".

Many of his 3,000 disciples established their own schools or held important positions in government after his death, endeavoring to promote and spread Confucian philosophy. Among them, 72 went on to live remarkable lives and became famous throughout Chinese history. The Chinese are often moved by stories of the Confucian disciples who considered him a father figure, remained loyal even during his 14-year exile, and mourned him for three years after his death. Zi Gong, one of the most famous and inspiring disciples, set up a hut near his master's grave and mourned him alone for another three years. He became an inspiring example for Chinese students in their behavior towards their teachers. The Temple and Cemetery of Confucius and the Kong Family was listed in 1994 as a UNESCO World Heritage Site and is today a popular tourist attraction.

Confucius' teachings were collected in the *Four Books* and *Five Classics* and contain the foundations of Confucianism. The *Four Books* consist of the *Analects*, *Mencius*, *Great Learning*, and *Doctrine of the Mean*. The *Five Classics* include *Classic of Poetry*, *Book of Documents*, *Book of Changes* (*Yi Jing*), *Book of Rites* and *Spring and Autumn Annals*. These five texts were compiled later during the Han dynasty and are part of the traditional Confucian canon. The *Classic of Music*, mentioned in some writings, is sometimes considered the sixth classic but was lost to history.

Confucius was a great humanist who advocated social harmony: "A true good man lives in harmony with his fellow men". In order to achieve this social harmony, he taught that one must cultivate three virtues: *li*, meaning "rituals and morality"; *ren*, meaning "humanism and benevolence"; and *dao*, meaning "the way of nature". The unity of the country, patriotism, peace and stability were the driving forces to which he dedicated his life. He initially wanted to use his political career to implement his ideals but, finding no success, he devoted the rest of his life to teaching.

Three concepts of Confucianism

Li ("rituals and morality") is the set of social rituals that govern the relationship between individuals and the conduct of ceremonies. This complex concept can be defined as the courtesies and standards of behavior that make up social morality. It covers all aspects of life, from the religious, governmental and family rites to the rules of social behavior.

Li also includes virtuous acts towards each other that demonstrate respect, tolerance, forgiveness, fidelity, devotion, trust and self-control. The Chinese preoccupation with saving face is dictated by compliance with *li*.

Li is also observed in cults rendered to deities and ancestors. One of Confucius' long-held civil service positions was that of providing funeral services which were generally long, strict and complex. Few people could manage such a responsibility.

Li reminds that each individual has an identity depending on the situation and must follow what they need to do in that identity. In this way, society can maintain its proper balance and harmony. For example, a man is a son in the presence of his father and must respect certain obligations and behavior. But in the presence of his own son, he is a father and the rituals and rites change accordingly. In the workplace, a person in front of their subordinates must assume their role as a superior and carry out the responsibilities of a superior. In front of their own superiors, however, they become subordinates and must adjust their conduct and obediently carry out their duties.

Li is described in the following Confucian texts: "To discipline one's desires, to regulate one's behavior and to make speech and actions conform to the norms of etiquette"; "Not to look, not to listen, not to speak and not to do what is not in conformity with *Li*"; and "A person who is apparently careful but who does not know how to be polite is tiring, a person who is cautious but who does not know how to be polite is cowardly, a person who is courageous but who does not know how to be polite is hurtful".

According to Confucius, "When everyone controls his actions and complies with *Li*, the whole world will return to benevolence. If everyone does his best to fulfill his own responsibilities, there would not be so many problems in society and the whole world would be at peace."

Li is an external constraint. Rules must be obeyed. *Ren* (benevolence) can be expressed through the rituals of *li*. Confucius believed that benevolence exists in every person.

For Confucius, it is not enough only to observe *li*. It is still necessary to show benevolence from the heart. *Ren* is at the center of *li*; without *ren*, rituals are like a rope that increasingly tightens around a person to make them uncomfortable. The practice of heartless rituals does not lead to a harmonious society.

Ren means benevolence, humanism and kindness. It should govern people's social and hierarchical relations with their rulers, relatives and friends. *Ren* has four fundamental elements: loyalty, fidelity, discernment and courage.

In Confucian doctrine, family relations are central in *ren*. Filial piety is a particularly important virtue: "Among the 100 human virtues, filial piety is above all others". Confucius believed that filial piety involved adopting a benevolent attitude towards and taking care of one's parents; showing courtesy and support; behaving well outside the home in order to bring honor to one's parents and ancestors; not being rebellious; ensuring male heirs and preserving fraternity among brothers; showing sadness at the illness and death of parents; and burying them and carrying out sacrifices after their death. "Only observe a man's intentions while his father is alive," Confucius said. "Only when his father is dead will his conduct reveal his true values. If during the three years of mourning he perpetuates these values towards his father, he will have shown great filial piety."

Hierarchy was crucial to society and the family. "The subjects serve the emperor, the son serves the father, the wife serves the husband," Confucius said. "When these three rules are respected, the world is in order; when these three rules are abandoned, the world is in chaos." According to him, "The emperor must treat his subjects with respect and benevolence, his subjects must serve the emperor with loyalty."

Confucius thought that practicing *ren* was not that difficult. When one person considers taking an action, they must first put themselves in the other's shoes. "What you do not wish for yourself, do not wish for others," Confucius said. "If you want to succeed, then you must first help others to succeed; if you want to excel, then you must help others to excel first."

According to him, *ren* can be revealed through education. *Ren* and *li* are the two fundamental pillars of a good person and a harmonious society.

A thinker and philosopher, Confucius spent his entire life in search of the truth about the human condition. He wanted to understand and decipher the *dao* to reach the ultimate truth. *Dao* in Chinese means "the way".

According to legend, the young Confucius sought out the teachings of Lao Zi, the founder of Taoism. Lao Zi criticized him for spending too much time educating people. He told the youngster that *dao* is everything that happens in the world—it is naturally predefined. Human nature is part of the predefined. Overwhelmed by Lao Zi's message, Confucius later explained his own understanding of *dao*.

He believed that everything in nature has its own path of development from which one cannot deviate. For example, the internal lines of each object are established. If we cut a tree, we may see the natural lines in the tree. If we cut a stone, we may observe its natural lines inside. A good carpenter must know how to cut wood along its natural grain. A good jade craftsman must carve raw jade according to its natural shape.

According to Confucius, our world has its own natural laws. We must observe and study phenomena in nature. These natural laws can guide our behavior so that we can reach the highest form of *li* and *ren*. Two of his quotes illustrate this: "Observe the phenomena of nature to gain knowledge, study the nature and essence of the world to understand human nature" and "The character that the sky gives to men is called nature, doing things according to nature is called *dao* and obeying *dao* leads to enlightenment".

One of the most representative Confucian concepts of *the dao* is the *Doctrine of the Mean* or *Zhong yong*, meaning "middle way". *Zhong* means "moderate" and *yong* means "ordinary". The goal is to maintain balance and harmony; this state of equilibrium is the universal path that all humans should pursue. "To achieve full personal realization is to attain the perfect Middle Way." The *Doctrine of the Mean* has been the central value of traditional Chinese culture, anchoring Chinese intellectual thinking for nearly 2,500 years and greatly contributing to the maintenance of imperial power.

In summary, in the Confucian vision, the variety of rituals practiced help maintain the social balance. Benevolence is at the heart of ritual because it is the only way to truly observe *li*. The *dao*, the natural law or order of the universe, makes it possible to reach a higher level of *li* and *ren*. One must observe and learn from these natural laws and then apply them to achieve harmony in the world.

Collectivism

The philosophy of Confucianism emphasizes the importance of relationships within a family and a society. Existing long before the arrival of Communism, a harmonious community and collectivist mindset are fundamental to Chinese society.

Under the influence of Confucianism, the Chinese see themselves as members of one big family. The notion of family extends to family, friends, businesses and the country and is reflected in small and big things. Take their meals, for example. Dishes are placed in the center of the table to be shared by all. Menus are available but not often used. Having a meal with many people in a joyful and friendly atmosphere contributes to a sense of sharing and a feeling of belonging. It gives the Chinese a sense of unity.

Whether in private or professional life, relationships are managed in the spirit of an extended family. The appellations such as brother, sister, uncle, aunt, grandfather and grandmother are used.

The Chinese language has a distinctly collective character. "We" and "our" are preferred to "I" and "my". People always talk about "our country", "our society" or "our family" even when just talking about themselves. The word "country" in Chinese is expressed as *guo jia*. The ideogram for *guo* means "the nation"; that for *jia* means "family", so for the Chinese their country is like their family. "We" is often pronounced in Chinese in a nuanced way: *wo men da jia*, which means "We, the big family".

Collectivism encourages the Chinese to conform to collective rules. This often happens through personal sacrifice. The interests of the group or country outweigh personal interests. People generally accept this without complaint. Confucianism's sense of duty and honor allows them to accept sacrifice for something greater. There are many examples of personal sacrifice for collective goals in China.

Each year, for the *Gāokǎo* examinations, the entire society is mobilized to ensure they run smoothly. Flights are redirected so that none overflies the examination locations. Funeral processions are diverted. Construction sites near schools can be temporarily closed. During exam days, police roadblocks are set up around the examination centers. No cars are allowed to honk their horns. During the 2008 Olympic Games, the route of the torch relay was modified to avoid disturbing the *Gāokǎo*.

The country's economic development has obliged tens of millions of families to leave their homes and to be relocated as a result of the construction of new infrastructure, such as new roads, railways, airports and water dams. During media interviews, these families often talk about their sadness and frustrations but also about their pride in being part of a great collective project.

China's one-child policy lasted from 1980 to 2015 and aimed to curb its growing population. A Chinese film *So Long, My Son* heartbreakingly describes the policy and its effects on relationships between members of a community, their feelings of powerlessness, sadness and willingness to sacrifice themselves for the good of the community. The film ends with an optimistic message: the lives of the people in this community have improved, friends have reconciled and people feel no resentment towards the State which imposed this policy on them.

During the current Covid-19 pandemic, the entire nation has adhered to the self-quarantine and drastic lockdown measures taken by the government. Without government intervention, millions of volunteers of various professions have been involved in the fight against the pandemic throughout China. In Wuhan alone, the city has registered 1.5 million volunteers coming from other Chinese cities, representing 14% of its permanent population. Local social workers have organized themselves voluntarily to enforce state-ordered containment measures. At the same time, they have provided or coordinated crucial services such as meal delivery, medical assistance (including psychological consultations) and liaison between communities and families. Many private companies, even some that were themselves struggling to survive, have made significant financial contributions to help communities in need. The Chinese collectivism showed its outstanding efficiency during the Covid-19 mass testing. In the city of Qingdao, with a population of 11 million, citywide screenings were completed in only five days.

An article in Bloomberg acknowledged that "The idea of sacrificing oneself for a greater national goal is deeply rooted in Chinese culture". In an article in *Time* magazine, columnist Jeffery Kluger, referring to China, wrote that "While pandemics will always be characterized by their randomness and ruthlessness and their power to cause suffering and death, the human response, when at its best, is defined by collective courage and compassion". Many Western and Asian experts have attributed the success of Covid-19 pandemic management in Asian countries to the strong centuries-old influence of Confucianism.

Chinese collectivism also manifests itself in the workplace. It is reflected in the organization, structure, relationships and commercial activities of Chinese companies.

Western companies in China often struggle to retain their best Chinese employees. It's not a question of offering good financial compensation or training opportunities. In fact, their working conditions generally surpass those of Chinese companies. But Chinese employees often say that they don't feel at home in Western companies as they do in Chinese companies. The problem is thus cultural.

In the Chinese workplace, organizing social activities to consolidate the team is part of a strong corporate culture. All employees participate in regular outings, such as hikes or hotpot and KTV evenings. Many Chinese companies have their own dining rooms where the majority of employees enjoy lunch together. During traditional festivals, birthdays and weddings hosted by an employee's family, their colleagues and managers are systematically invited. Everyone gives those red envelopes. In China, colleagues become often personal friends and spend a lot of time together.

The Chinese traditionally take post-lunch naps. This custom is adopted in Chinese companies, especially in traditional companies and those located inland, and many provide the necessary facilities.

To understand Chinese collectivism, we can also look at the power structure of Chinese companies. Most operate with one important person (a president) at the top and a group of vice presidents just below. This structure ensures that everyone works towards a common goal and that no one, except the president, has too much power. Since their main purpose is to fulfill their responsibilities, Chinese employees tend to get involved wherever they are needed and work towards a common goal. This organization encourages the group dynamic and emphasizes strong relationships between colleagues.

The need to save face also plays an important role in Chinese collectivism. Before suggesting an innovative idea, Chinese employees attribute the idea to the group to which they belong. If the idea is successful, the whole group is rewarded. If it is rejected or harms the company, which leads to a loss of face, the employees continue to demonstrate solidarity so that they mutually support each other and no one loses face. In this way, the interests of the group are protected.

One of the fundamental principles of collectivism is that the individual gives up personal interests and shares resources to facilitate the interests of the group. Many Chinese employees work overtime every week, considering this to be normal and their contribution to the group.

Meetings in Chinese companies also illustrate this collectivism. Internal meetings can often be long, arduous, even aimless. Everyone has to say something. The purpose is not necessarily to get things done but rather to make everyone participate. All members are in the same room, whether the meeting has merit or not, and they work as a team. Most of the time, employees leave the meeting muttering to themselves that the exercise was a waste of time, while the person in charge of the meeting likely thinks that the team connected meaningfully.

"Ingroup" and "outgroup" cultural identity is also prominent in China. Groups can be formed according to different motives: place of origin, family network, the company for which the members work, social status, etc. The members of a group show solidarity in private and professional affairs. They can benefit from important advantages offered by the group. In the workplace, favors are often granted to members of the ingroup, especially in recruitment and promotion.

In return, the members have duties towards the group. Executives leaving a company often take their entire team with them to the new employer. Relationships with colleagues in ingroups being cooperative and supportive, these members can be cold and distrustful towards the outgroups, the result of a sense of duty and loyalty to the ingroup.

Collectivism also influences the behavior of Chinese consumers. They like to get information from their friends or family members. Preferring to get advice from members of the ingroup, they are reassured when products have been tested by people they trust. In the meantime, this satisfies the ingroup's conformity when they buy the same products.

Collectivism is also reflected in consumer choice. Although Confucianism teaches the Chinese to be frugal, attention to the family or community must be emphasized. For most Chinese, the practice of frugality is for oneself and generosity is for the community. The purchase of gifts accounts for a very large share of Chinese consumer spending and its total amount increases year after year. The development of products that can be offered as gifts, particularly those based on traditional culture, has grown enormously in recent years. Gifts for the elderly, children and women are extremely popular. The offer of gifts is one of the main reasons why Chinese consumers are heavy buyers of Western luxury products.

In corporate business development, collectivism is a unique asset. During the Ming and Qing dynasties, commercial gangs (*shang bang*) were very active parts of urban life. One significant feature was their formation into regional collectivist unions to cope with social, political and economic difficulties. Today, this practice continues in the Chinese market. Businessmen group together according to their place of origin, often from the same village, which facilitates relationship building. Coming from the same place, speaking the same dialect and loving the same style of cuisine fosters a sense of unity with their native region. Businesses belonging to the same *shang bang* work together by coordinating, helping each other and granting each other favorable conditions.

In addition, in order to integrate business resources effectively, companies in the same industry group together, establishing internal rules, deciding who is responsible for the transaction, for transportation, for product integrity, etc. By sharing more resources, they gain a competitive advantage, achieve greater growth, and increase their ambition.

Today, there are three major *shang bang*: the Zhe, located in Zhejiang province (one of its representatives is Jack Ma); the Yue, located in Guangdong province (one of its representatives is Ma Huateng, CEO of Tencent); and the Min, located in Fujian province (one of its representatives is Cao Dewang the Chinese king of glass manufacturing).

Western companies advocate a spirit of individualism, so it may be difficult for them to adopt or approve of Chinese collectivism. But understanding this concept and its implications is the first step toward optimally adapting their operations to the Chinese market.

Authoritarian and humanistic leadership

Confucianism advocates a society with hierarchical human relations in which both authoritarian and humanistic leadership must be applied. Traditional Chinese leadership consists of three key elements: authoritarianism, benevolence and morality. In the business context, it is a paternalistic leadership style with strong authority combined with benevolent consideration for employees.

In business, the authority of the Chinese leader is reflected in different ways. The concept of *li* (being polite and courteous) is observed in the hierarchical professional relationship. Subordinates use honorary titles towards their superiors and in everyday language they address them with the superiors' title preceding their last name: President Xi, Chairman Mao, Minister Deng, Director Li, etc. This conveys the proper respect.

Under the influence of the traditional hierarchical system, there is a large power gap between the top superior and his subordinates in Chinese enterprises. This gap is much greater in Chinese companies than in Western companies. A Chinese business leader is often the only person to make important decisions. Although he also has to listen to the advice of various people in order to conform to democratic functioning, frequently asking his subordinates for advice in a decision-making process can be considered a sign of incompetence. As a result, Chinese employees generally expect clear instructions from their superiors and are less likely to express their opinions or make proposals. Western-style employee empowerment can be interpreted by Chinese employees as a lack of competence or laziness on the part of the leader.

Where a superior and an employee disagree, the employee is expected to submit to the superior. Publicly disputing a superior can be considered treason.

In Chinese companies, respect for social rules and for superiors and elders is accepted as part of the natural order, making it easy for management to exercise control. Many Chinese companies do so, based on loyalty, trust and seniority. Respecting these values is taken into account when appraising employees' careers. Loyalty to one's superiors, for example, is considered an important criterion for promotion.

Chinese managers simultaneously feel responsible not only for their subordinates' work performance but also for their personal well-being, and are committed to helping them to deal with concerns such as housing, healthcare or personal conflicts. For example, a manager will take an interest in news about an employee's family or often be concerned about an employee's marital relationship, or will participate in employees' family celebrations or funerals.

Chinese leaders are required to do their best to get closer to their employees and may even share their bonuses to thank them for their efforts and support.

Chinese leaders are not, in the interest of saving face, supposed to criticize their employees in public, otherwise they could be perceived as incompetent.

To maintain harmony, Chinese leaders tend to treat all employees equally and fairly in all circumstances. There are a large number of family-owned businesses in China whose leaders often have the difficult task of treating all family members and their close or distant friends equally. They often have to be more severe with their close relatives, to set an example of equality, than with more distant ones. Mismanagement can sometimes seriously disrupt the smooth running of the business. These leaders, who are like father figures in a family, prefer to avoid layoffs. They must constantly show Confucian benevolence towards their employees and be involved in solving their personal and professional problems.

In state-owned companies, the management control is usually centralized and personalized. Controllers sent by the provincial authority carry out audits of companies in subordinate cities. Audits of managers can be through formal or informal processes and, when it comes to the well-being of the people under their charge, the consequences can be severe. Following the fight against the Covid-19 pandemic, 3,000 Chinese officials from central and regional government were removed from their posts in 2020 due to inefficiencies or mistakes in handling the crisis.

Many Chinese business managers have undertaken MBA studies in the United States or Europe. Although the influence of the Western management system is gradually increasing in China, companies are still strongly influenced by the traditional culture. The paternalistic leadership style remains predominant and Chinese employees accept it for the moment. Nevertheless, it is important to distinguish between state-owned and private companies. State-owned companies remain focused on altruism stemming from Confucianism. The private sector, on the other hand, is more attracted to the Western management model, considering it more efficient and effective.

Conflict management

A popular Chinese proverb holds that "One must melt a great conflict into a small one and then melt the small one into nothing". The Chinese people use it as a daily mantra. The search for harmony, the maintenance of the relationship at all costs, the saving of face, and the adoption of mediation constitute the predominant model of Chinese conflict management.

The Chinese don't perceive conflicts as a communication problem but rather as disruptive to harmony. Restoring harmony in interpersonal relationships is the ultimate goal.

Saving face is crucial in the traditional approach to conflict management in China. Most Chinese tend to view direct confrontation as unpleasant, undesirable and to be avoided. For example, a couple in conflict will seek reconciliation at all costs, no matter which parties are involved in helping them. Whether the conflict is resolved by the couple themselves, by parental intervention or by social pressure, reconciliation is the priority at any cost.

Chinese consumer behavior demonstrates another example of avoidance. It is an unwritten rule that peace be the most precious thing in a relationship. Chinese consumers rarely litigate infringements of their rights, preferring instead to vent their frustrations with family, friends or colleagues. Recent economic developments and increased consumption are slowly—very slowly—beginning to change this non-confrontational mindset.

While conflicts are inevitable, the Chinese strongly favor mediation. *Shuo he*, meaning "to talk about peace", underpins the mediator's role. Peace at any price is the immediate objective of mediation. For the Chinese, recourse to a mediator allows harmony to be preserved, avoids losing a friendly relationship, and contributes to the creation of a pleasant atmosphere for cooperation and future negotiations.

Seniority in age is a highly sought-after quality in a mediator because senior age in China is linked to credibility. Ideal mediators also come from the ranks of the senior corporate management or government. These people of power are considered the most competent in finding the fairest solution and their recommendations are generally accepted and implemented at the end of the talks.

In Chinese culture, all these avoidance and mediation-seeking approaches are part of *li*. The Chinese prefer *xian li hou bing*, meaning "peaceful measures before using force" or "diplomacy before violence".

Chinese employers usually try to avoid a formal process because it is time-consuming and costly. To unilaterally terminate an employee, the employer would have to establish legitimate reasons or the termination would be considered illegal, in which case the employee can demand a substantial severance package or even reinstatement.

In the event of disagreement, an "informal" labor dispute becomes "formal": one of the parties, usually the employee, files a lawsuit which is then approved by the Labor Office after examination of the file. Many informal and formal interventions are thus offered by this Office with the aim of encouraging the amicable settlement of disputes. The Office encourages the parties to resolve their dispute amicably via pre-arbitration and arbitration. The arbitrators are often retired government employees experienced in Chinese labor law and dispute resolution.

At the end of each hearing, the arbitrator invites the parties to talk privately under his supervision in an effort to reach an informal resolution, guiding the negotiations and coaxing either party to accept the other's settlement offer.

If the parties reach an agreement in a guided arbitration, the arbitrator issues a formal ruling. If the parties do not reach an agreement, they can appeal to the civil courts where the judge will again appoint an arbitrator to review the case. The employer and the employee are again encouraged to resolve their dispute through mediation rather than litigation.

If the parties still cannot agree, the civil court judge takes over the case and pushes for a compromise, failing which the judge will render judgment.

Chinese authorities indirectly encourage arbitrators and judges to resolve civil disputes through the widely favored compromise. For the employer, this usually means offering a severance package to the employee. Litigation, which is a public procedure, is disapproved of because Chinese culture prefers to keep disputes out of the public eye.

It follows that disputes between Chinese companies and foreign companies are similarly handled.

As part of the ongoing reform of the Chinese legal system, in September 2019 the Chinese government encouraged the deepening of diversified dispute resolution mechanisms for companies. It called for increased use of civil mediation, administrative mediation, lawyers' mediation, industrial mediation, professional mediation and mediation by chambers of commerce. This allows for maximum integration of resources, rational division of labor and improved efficiency. (65)

Fusion of Chinese and Western culture

Zhong yong, the "middle way", encompasses three notions: moderation, simplicity and acceptance. The fusion of Chinese and Western culture in modern China manifests this "middle way".

For thousands of years, agriculture has been fundamental to China's economic growth. China ignored the first two Industrial Revolutions in the West and was in the process of starting its reform on economic development when the Western world entered the advanced phase of the third Industrial Revolution. It is therefore obvious that industrialization and learning from and accepting Western culture are very important to China. Integrating Western products and services into its business ecosystem benefits the country. The Chinese are fascinated by Western culture. This phenomenon continues in parallel with a renewed interest in traditional Chinese culture.

As a result of its successful economic growth, China has won greater collective cultural confidence and awareness.

In recent years, China has begun to incorporate the long-neglected traditional Chinese culture into its education system covering all levels: pre-school, basic, vocational, higher and continuing. Initial efforts are concentrated on creating the teaching materials and curriculum. Strengthening training for all teachers and improving the overall level of educational institutions' staff are also priorities. Promoting Chinese opera, calligraphy, traditional art and sports in schools is emphasized.

In its efforts to restore its ancient culture, China has been striving to recover more and more of its lost cultural artifacts scattered around the world. Various methods are used to search for these artifacts: donations, bilateral law enforcement cooperation, litigation, diplomatic negotiation, and repurchase. China has so far signed 23 bilateral agreements with other countries. Italy and Greece are known to hold many ancient Chinese artifacts; the United States and Australia have purchased most of them; and many were returned to China in 2019.

The renewed Chinese interest in their traditional culture is increasing, expressed by a willingness to return to the source. Traditional culture has gained ground, especially in the form of entertainment. Television programs featuring music, literature and treasures from national museums are very popular. This phenomenon affects Chinese people of all ages. Young artists actively participate in these programs and develop more reflection in their creations based on traditional culture. Young Chinese audiences are burgeoning.

China's booming cultural industry is seen in the press and publishing, television and cinema, live performances, Internet and mobile communication, games, advertising, exhibitions and various production activities, and design.

A return to traditional Chinese values is also evolving with renewed confidence in the creation of commercial design products. Not so long ago, China had no design brand of its own but Chinese designers are increasingly committed to giving new meaning to "Made in China" in their creations which are linked to tradition and craftsmanship. Shaped by the cultural heritage of the Middle Kingdom and identified by quests for original concepts, the aesthetic of modern Chinese fashion is deeply linked to the country's ancient roots.

China has one of the world's most dynamic cultural and creative environments. Its domestic cultural market is booming and characterized by an increase in the purchasing power of the urban middle class, which spends 10–14% of its income on education, culture and leisure.

The country intends to make its cultural industry a pillar of the national economy by modernizing its industrial structure, promoting major brands and stimulating consumption. Its political will to restore and revive traditional Chinese culture is strong. As a result, a genuine culture industry is developing, which today accounts for 4% of GDP. According to an official forecast, this figure should reach 6 to 7% by 2023. China has experienced strong online and offline momentum in the development of its cultural industry. In the context of resuming its work after the pandemic, the online culture industry is among those that have embarked on a new growth expansion.

Jean-Pierre Raffarin, the former French Prime Minister, is very much involved in the promotion of Franco-Chinese economic and trade relations. He has supported thousands of French companies to work in the Chinese market. His 50 years of experience with China make him an undisputed top-level expert in the field. In his latest book, *China—the Great Paradox*, he wrote that "China seeks to assemble together the terms of an alternative, when Europeans want to oppose them; Europeans tend to think in *or*, when the Chinese tend to think in *and*".

China has been looking to the West for 40 years. Accepting and including numerous concepts from the United States and Europe is reflected in its efforts to internationalize the country.

China is proudly integrating the English language in public facilities at the same level as its national language. In all newly built infrastructure, traffic instructions are displayed in Chinese and English. Announcements on both coastal and inland public transportation, including subways and trains, are also in

Chinese and English. Chinese entertainment programs (movies, TV series, concerts, etc.) are increasingly subtitled in English. English language learning has been a priority for the younger generation for decades. Fluency in English is almost mandatory and has become one of the selection criteria in the job market. In daily conversation, more and more English words—*OK, bye-bye, dear, get, hold*—are being adopted and integrated into Chinese sentences, especially by young people.

More and more Chinese lead a westernized lifestyle. Everything Western is described in Chinese as *yang qi*, a compliment meaning "the energy of the West".

The Chinese eat American or European meals, wear Western brands and celebrate Western holidays such as Valentine's Day and Halloween. China is the world's leading producer of Christmas garlands and baubles. In ten years, Christmas markets have appeared in all major Chinese cities and it is not only Westerners who visit them—most visitors to these markets are Chinese families who have a taste for festivities and a curiosity about other cultures.

Today, the Chinese upper class wants to consume not only Western products but also Western social and cultural experiences. This explains its growing appetite for acquiring Western etiquette. Finishing schools are flourishing in China's major cities, teaching the Chinese Western table manners and how to behave in Western high society.

The Chinese love for Western classical music is not new. It dates back to the end of the Qing dynasty at the beginning of the 20th century when Western missionaries brought musical instruments, including a harpsichord, as gifts to the emperor. After the 1911 Revolution, several Chinese musicians left the country to study in Europe and returned with knowledge that enabled them to form symphony orchestras in several major Chinese cities, much to the delight of the population.

Learning classical music in China is taken very seriously. It is estimated that between 30 and 100 million children study either piano, violin, or both. A student can be admitted to a Chinese university with a lower average if they master a musical instrument. Conservatories are overcrowded and ultra-modern concert halls and professional orchestras are flourishing. European classical music arouses real emotion among the Chinese. Young people rush to concerts and some keep a picture of Mozart in their wallet. Piano sellers resemble car dealerships where young people spontaneously play recitals on pianos of various international brands.

China's policy of internationalization is evident in numerous radical changes to its laws. As soon as it was awarded Expo 2010 in Shanghai, it immediately began cracking down on drunk driving. The culture of drinking hard liquor at business meals was one of the main causes of road accidents, which have drastically decreased. New laws were also passed to combat pollution, smoking in public places, and corruption of public officials. The Chinese government viewed these problems as detrimental to the country's international image and which prevented it from complying with international standards.

In commerce, the Chinese film market has become the world's largest, ahead of its North American competitor, and is becoming an essential step in the commercial strategies of Western studios. Many major Western productions owe much of their worldwide success to their popularity in Chinese cinemas. These productions sometimes even serve as a lifeline for feature films which struggle in Europe and America. China is an essential market for Hollywood studios. American blockbusters make a killing there, while American superhero and science fiction films do well at the box office, often ranking second and third in China's film ratings.

The Chinese view the consumption of Western wine as a mark of social status. French, Chilean and Australian wines are favorites, with French and Australian wines each making up a third of Chinese wine imports until the end of 2019. Western wine consumption is growing steadily—it is estimated that by 2025 the average per capita consumption will be double that of today.

Dairy products are not part of traditional Chinese food and the Chinese are not used to the taste of Western cheeses. However, cheese has become a new growth point for the dairy sector in China. Thanks to the growing popularity of Western cuisine, the Chinese are becoming increasingly receptive to Western food tastes. According to Euromonitor International, the London-based market research firm, cheese sales in China, including processed and unprocessed cheeses, are expected to reach USD 1.44 billion by 2023, 44.7% higher than current sales levels.

Finally, China's coffee market is still in its infancy but growing rapidly, encouraged by the younger generation that converges on independent coffee shops and an urban middle class that is sensitive to Western influences. Coffee was historically a luxury product but has recently become more accessible and offers a taste of the Western lifestyle. International Coffee Organization statistics indicate that, in a country whose culture is inextricably linked to tea, the demand for coffee has grown at double-digit annual rates over the past 20 years.

Jacques Attali, the French economic and social theorist, entrepreneur, writer, former senior civil servant, who served as an advisor to former French President François Mitterrand, said in an interview with *Forbes* magazine in 2019 that "I don't believe that China is an imperialist power with a desire for world domination. It is not in its culture, traditions or interests. Nevertheless, China is going to become a very great power. For example, its presence will necessarily grow in Africa to ensure its resource supplies. But it is a power that does not seek to indoctrinate the world. The Chinese way of life is already very westernized. Indeed, China has swallowed a large number of Western concepts during the 20th century that it must now digest".

Attali's view seems fair and insightful. One of the characteristics of this country of Confucianism has always been its capacity for acceptance. The principle of *zhong yong* allowed China to have a strong sense of inclusiveness. It has embraced Western culture without restraint in its recent economic development. While valuing its cultural heritage, its thirst for Western culture remains enormous. This feverish fascination has slowed down as a result of the geopolitical challenges during the Covid-19 pandemic but the Chinese government has affirmed its will to continue to open the country to the world. Multilateralism is one of the main objectives of its policy.

Conclusion

The Forbidden City in Beijing is the most emblematic monument of Chinese tradition. Two large placards have been hung on the facade of the building's main entrance since the founding of the PRC seventy years ago. One reads "Long live the People's Republic of China"; the other reads "Long live the unity of the peoples of the world". They demonstrate the Chinese vision in accordance with its culture of unity influenced by Confucianism.

China has been pursuing this idealism for 70 years. Today, China's primary concern is the elimination of poverty in the country through economic development. It hopes, through the BRI, to broaden development in a globalized world. By sharing its know-how in infrastructure construction, it wishes to establish friendly ties with the member countries of the BRI. In 2013, President Xi Jinping proposed for the first time a Chinese concept for the world called "building a community with a shared future for mankind" and called for creating a world of peace with close cooperation and equality in the economic, cultural and political spheres. All this is part of his "China Dream".

To realize this dream, China has a long-term global strategy best understood by *Wéi qí*, an ancient encirclement board game known in the West as Go. According to legend, the game dates back 4,000 years when the tribal chief Rao supposedly used stones to teach his son the art of survival. A more documented origin appears in the *Annals* where Confucius mentions *Wéi qí* as early as the 5th century BC. Historical records from the 3rd century BC also mention this strategy game. Buddhist monks helped spread it to Japan and Korea nearly 1,000 years ago. In the 16th century, the game was introduced to the West thanks to the exchanges between the countries of the Far East and Europe. Traces of the first western incursions of this game can be found in Matteo Ricci's diary (1582–1610) and in Alvarez Semedo's *Relatione della Grande Monarchia della* Cina, published in 1643. Western federations of the game were organized as early as 1920 in the United States, then in France around 1969.

Wéi qí is popular in China and Asia because of its simple rules and rich combinations. There are 361 black and white stones representing 361 days and placed on a square board with 19 horizontal and 19 vertical squares. The board symbolizes the earth. One player opens the game with a black stone. Each player then positions their stones with the objective of surrounding a larger total area of the board with their stones. Limiting the opponent's advance and capturing their stones is the key tactic in occupying more territory. The general strategy is to expand one's territory and knock out the opponent's weaknesses. The winner is determined by counting each player's surrounded territory and the number of captured stones. The player with the highest number is the winner.

In ancient China, *Wéi qí* was one of the four fundamental arts that one had to master to be considered educated and accomplished. The other three were *Gǔ qín* (the Chinese zither), Chinese calligraphy and Chinese painting. In the imperial court, the emperor often selected talents by playing *Wéi qí* with them. This allowed him to determine their character, potential and vison of the world.

Wéi qí stones are identical and unmarked. The simple, ordinary and contrasting black and white symbolize the yin and yang of ancient Chinese philosophy.

The goal of the game is not to fight or eliminate the opponent but to occupy maximum territory, marshal survival resources, and achieve harmony with the opponent. It is a game of strategy that requires a global and long-term vision. Patience and excellent judgment are essential player qualities. The game's main strategies are illustrated in *Ten Golden Rules of Wéi qí*, written by Wang Zhixin, a famous poet during the Tang dynasty and one of the best *Wéi qí* players of his time.

China's economic development policy is often seen as being inspired by this game. Chinese entrepreneurs also apply its principles in their business development. Writing in the *Harvard Business Review*, a group of strategy experts demonstrated how the Chinese multinationals Alibaba, Huawei and Vanke have put *Wéi qí* principles into practice in their companies' strategic development. (66)

Alibaba's Jack Ma has often mentioned his taste for the game, saying that he played it a lot in university. He explained how he had aimed wide in time and space and used the game's principles to develop his business. One of his key strategies was to look for the most valuable positioning.

By applying the checkerboard edge principle, Huawei not only relied on local market demand but also on initial activity which was easily accessible in terms of the skills and resources to be deployed. Huawei gradually moved towards the center, towards its long-term strategic objective of becoming a leading player in the mobile telephone industry by playing the differentiation and international card.

Another key strategic maneuver in *Wéi qí* is to know when to give up and not give in to greed. Marking a turning point in its development strategy, the Chinese real estate giant Vanke was able to implement this principle.

This ancestral Chinese thinking, realized in *Wéi qí*, inspires millions of Chinese companies in their development strategy, business management and relational vision with their partners.

*****

Many international experts and personalities predict that China will take the lead role in the global economy. It is in the process of moving from a position of follower to one of decision-maker. While its management of the pandemic is controversial in the West, it was one of the first countries to initiate economic recovery. Kishore Mahbubani, Singapore's former ambassador to the U.S. and former president of the United Nations Security Council, said that the world was amazed at how effectively China had stopped a very dangerous virus and strengthened its position in tomorrow's world order.

According to the International Monetary Fund's (IMF) latest *World Economic Outlook*, China remained the only economy in the world to post positive growth in 2020, with its GDP growing by 2.3%. Thanks to a faster-than-expected recovery, China's growth will accelerate to 8.2% in 2021. IMF Chief Economist Gita Gopinath also said that China was improving global figures and that "without China, the cumulative global growth for 2020 and 2021 would be negative". Bloomberg used the same IMF data to conclude that China's share of global growth is expected to rise from 26.8 percent in 2021 to 27.7 percent in 2025, and thus would be higher than the U.S. share. The United Nations Conference on Trade and Development released a report on January 24th, 2021, confirming that China was the largest recipient of foreign direct investment in 2020: USD 163 billion in inflows, compared to USD 134 billion attracted by the United States.

***

China's tomorrow is taking shape. The first Chinese five-year plan was launched in 1950 and its provisional 14th five-year plan was announced in October 2020. The first priority of this plan is the "dual circulation" strategy that places a greater focus on China's domestic market, or internal circulation, and less reliance on its export-oriented development strategy, or external circulation, with its continuing development. Some incorrectly interpreted this as a sign that Beijing was turning its back on the outside world, but the plan clearly states that policies must help unlock the full potential of the domestic market, helping businesses to provide better-quality goods and services to stimulate domestic demand. At the same time, Beijing promised better access to foreign investors and encouraged Chinese companies to increase trade with other countries. The Chinese government wants its opening to the international market "to be on a larger scale, in more sectors and at a deeper level".

Negotiated since 2013, the EU-China Comprehensive Agreement on Investment was concluded on December 30, 2020. The European objective is to make the Chinese market open up further to investments from EU companies. Johnathan Arnott, former member of the European Parliament, gave his analysis: "For its part, the EU is clearly satisfied with this agreement. The EU has received what it considers to be a generous offer from China for better access to the Chinese market. Much of what China will gain from this agreement is likely to be stability: the assurance that the objectives will not be misplaced and that China can plan for the long term. When long-term prosperity and short-term gains conflict, China tends to choose the former while the nature of Western governments requires choosing the latter." (67)

The second priority in the provisional 14th five-year plan is "innovation", which was mentioned 47 times in the draft proposal. The new plan places innovation at the heart of China's future plans. China aims to make major breakthroughs in core technologies and crucial areas and to become a world leader in innovation. Many predict strong political will to increase spending in the coming years in emerging sectors such as biotechnology, semiconductors and new energy vehicles.

"Green growth" is another focus area of this five-year plan. In the draft proposal, there are no rigid GDP targets for the next five years, while "green growth" is mentioned 19 times, a sign that the country continues to encourage local leaders to look beyond GDP as a key performance indicator and instead focus on sustainable, low-carbon growth models. (68)

China's new infrastructure initiative, announced in May 2020, includes seven key areas: 5G networks, industrial Internet, intercity transportation and rail systems, data centers, AI, ultra-high voltage power transmission, and charging stations for new energy vehicles. To ensure nationwide 5G coverage, between five and 5.5 million 5G base stations are expected to be built by 2025. Other major projects have been announced for the period up to 2025: build three to five world-class industrial Internet platforms to help one million enterprises achieve their digital transformation; build a massive but undisclosed number of large data centers, supercenters and edge data centers to meet the growing national demand for data storage; build 20 innovative AI pilot areas across the country by 2023; and launch up to 16 projects to build extra-high voltage power lines, including power transformer extensions and new converter stations.

Analysts at the China Center for Information Industry Development, a think tank affiliated with the Chinese government, and Haitong International Securities Group estimate that investment in new infrastructure projects is expected to be between USD 1,430 billion and USD 2,510 billion by 2025. (69)

Compared to the increase in state-led investment in traditional infrastructure following the 2008 global financial crisis, the biggest distinction in the 2020 post-pandemic stimulus package is that the Chinese government is now much more dependent on market forces and private investment. The 14th five-year plan, officially approved in March 2021, foresees many more opportunities for the various stakeholders allowing them to participate in this next phase of China's development. A large number of sectors will consist of private investment and will offer interesting opportunities for foreign investment.

***

We live in a time of multiple changes and dramatic upheavals. The world is at a historical turning point. The Western economic sector is facing unprecedented challenges. At the dawn of its growing influence, understanding China accurately is urgent. Mastering the Chinese business culture should be a priority. Assimilating Chinese business strategy, as taught in *The Art of War* and played in *Wéi qí*, is paramount. For Western companies, applying this knowledge in their relations with their Chinese partners is critical to achieving long-term business success with China.

Author's biography

Qingshun Zou was born in Beijing and grew up in Guangzhou in southern China. She was educated in Canada, completing her studies in business at a Canadian university in Nova Scotia. Nostalgia for her homeland and stimulating encounters in the West ignited in her an interest in both cultures.

Having started her career in the Swiss watch industry, Qingshun received training in marketing at Swatch AG before turning to entrepreneurship. After having successfully developed several companies in Switzerland and China, she was CEO of the Swiss subsidiary of a European pharmaceutical group for more than 15 years.

A Swiss citizen, Qingshun is a professional in international business development. As a business consultant, she offers her know-how in a multicultural environment, leading a training program entitled "Decoding the Chinese business culture" in partnership with the Geneva Business Management University. Founder of the company Sino Swiss Business Alliance Development Sàrl, she supports European and Chinese companies from various industries in their business projects. Her activities extend to cross-cultural management training and advisory on business strategy, management and development.

Inspired by Western culture, she has been an amateur musician for 15 years. With her enthusiasm for and sensitivity to Chinese and Western cultures, Qingshun is a board member of the prestigious Geneva International Music Competition, founded in 1939.

www.qingshunzou.com

Bibliography

1. 2019 全国高考报名人数破千万，比去年增加 56 万人. [Online] China Education Online, 06 07, 2019. https://gaokao.eol.cn/news/201906/t20190607_1662781.shtml.

2. Pourquoi la musique classique explose-t-elle en Chine ? [Online] France Musique, 03 29, 2019. https://www.francemusique.fr/actualite-musicale/pourquoi-la-musique-classique-explose-en-chine-71257.

3. 2019 年中国出国留学人数、留学归国人数及留学意向地区分布占比. [Online] China Industry Information, 01 13, 2020. https://www.chyxx.com/industry/202001/828614.html.

4. Number of International Students in the United States Hits All-Time High. [Online] The Power of International Education, 11 18, 2019. https://www.iie.org/Why-IIE/Announcements/2019/11/Number-of-International-Students-in-the-United-States-Hits-All-Time-High.

5. Homepage. [Online] Open Doors Data, 11 2020. https://opendoorsdata.org/.

6. Research Special Reports and Analyses. [Online] Opendoorsdata.org, 12 2020. https://opendoorsdata.org/services/research-special-reports-and-analyses/#:~:text=Economic%20Impact%20of%20International%20Students,the%20U.S.%20Department%20of%20Commerce..

7. Jacques, Martin. From Follower To Leader: The Story Of China's Rise. [Online] YouTube, 09 21, 2020. https://www.youtube.com/watch?v=Psyy4KqEKtA&t=4s.

8. Li, Jianxin and Liu, Mei. 我国少数民族人口现状及变化特点. [Online] 01 20, 2020. http://cssn.cn/mzx/shwh/202001/t20200120_5081504.shtml.

9. Number of Schools,Educational Personnel and Full-time Teachers by Type and Level - Number of Students of Formal Education by Type and Level. [Online] 12 2020. http://www.moe.gov.cn/s78/A03/moe_560/jytjsj_2019/qg/202006/t20200611_464804.html.

10. L'enseignement supérieur. [Online] China.org.cn, 12 2020. http://french.china.org.cn/archives/chine2006/txt/2006-11/27/content_2265704.htm.

11. Le taux brut de scolarisation dans l'enseignement supérieur en Chine atteint 48,1% en 2018. [Online] Xinhuanet, 07 27, 2019. http://french.xinhuanet.com/2019-07/27/c_138262477.htm.

12. Chinese university graduates rise exponentially, have diverse career options. [Online] Xinhuanet, 06 24, 2019. http://www.xinhuanet.com/english/2019-06/24/c_138169311.htm.

13. La Chine a fait un grand pas en avant dans l'éducation au cours des 70 dernières années. [Online] Xinhuanet, 09 08, 2019. http://french.xinhuanet.com/2019-09/08/c_138375518.htm#:~:text=Xinhua%20Multim%C3%A9dia-,La%20Chine%20a%20fait%20un%20grand%20pas%20en%20avant%20dans,cours%20des%2070%20derni%C3%A8res%20ann%C3%A9es&text=L'%C3%A9ducation%20professionnelle%20a%20%C3%A9galem.

14. 中国的社会保障. [Online] People's Republic of China, 04 20, 2012. http://www.gov.cn/test/2012-04/20/content_2118401.htm.

15. 中国老龄人口已达 2.5 亿 当你老了，如何养老. [Online] Xinhuanet, 04 11, 2019. http://www.xinhuanet.com/fortune/2019-04/11/c_1124350926.htm.

16. Homepage. [Online] People's Republic of China.

17. 超八成！经济普查显示我国私营企业数量占比提升. [Online] People's Republic of China, 11 27, 2019. http://www.gov.cn/guowuyuan/2019-11/27/content_5456477.htm.

18. 经济普查显示我国私营企业数量占比提升，达 84.1%. [Online] Sina.com.cn, 11 27, 2019. https://finance.sina.com.cn/roll/2019-11-27/doc-iihnzhfz2129019.shtml.

19. Vivienne. Chine : le secteur privé contribue considérablement à la croissance économique. [Online] China.org.cn, 03 06, 2018. http://french.china.org.cn/business/txt/2018-03/06/content_50670276.htm.

20. China's foreign trade hit \$4.6 trillion in 2019. [Online] CGTN, 01 14, 2020. https://news.cgtn.com/news/2020-01-14/China-s-foreign-trade-hit-4-6-tln-in-2019-NdB8lVuPba/index.html.

21. *World Trade Statistical Review 2020.* s.l. : World Trade Organization, 2020.

22. Workman, Daniel. China's Top 10 Exports. [Online] Worldstopexports, 12 2020. http://www.worldstopexports.com/chinas-top-10-exports/.

23. —. China's Top 10 Imports. [Online] Worldstopexports, 12 2020. http://www.worldstopexports.com/chinas-top-10-imports/.

24. —. China's Top Trading Partners. [Online] Worldstopexports, 12 2020. http://www.worldstopexports.com/chinas-top-import-partners/.

25. China's trade with major economies accelerates in September as global economy reopens. [Online] CGTN, 10 13, 2020. https://news.cgtn.com/news/2020-10-13/China-s-foreign-trade-up-0-7-in-first-3-quarters-of-2020-Uy4ABZef5e/index.html.

26. Leverage RCEP to turbocharge the renaissance of Asia. [Online] CGTN, 11 16, 2020. https://news.cgtn.com/news/2020-11-16/Leverage-RCEP-to-turbocharge-the-renaissance-of-Asia-VrvAPQM6RO/index.html.

27. Qi, Xijia. Huawei to top world's 5G smartphone output in 2020: report. [Online] Globaltimes, 07 22, 2020. https://www.globaltimes.cn/content/1195363.shtml.

28. Chen, Qingqing and Fan, Lingzhi. Shenzhen becomes 1st Chinese city to realize full-scale 5G deployment. [Online] Globaltimes, 08 17, 2020. https://www.globaltimes.cn/content/1197950.shtml.

29. China has over 700,000 5G base stations : official. [Online] Xinhuanet, 11 27, 2020. http://www.xinhuanet.com/english/2020-11/27/c_139545480.htm#:~:text=GUANGZHOU%2C%20Nov.,year%2C%20an%20official%20said%20Thursday..

30. The history of Artificial Intelligence (AI) in China. [Online] Daxueconsulting, 01 17, 2020. https://daxueconsulting.com/history-china-artificial-intelligence/.

31. Pizzuto, Luca, et al. How China will help fuel the revolution in autonomous vehicles. [Online] Mckinsey, 12 2020. https://www.mckinsey.com/industries/automotive-and-assembly/our-insights/how-china-will-help-fuel-the-revolution-in-autonomous-vehicles.

32. Shanghai hosts 2019 World Artificial Intelligence Conference to boost innovation. [Online] Xinhuanet, 08 29, 2019. http://www.xinhuanet.com/english/2019-08/29/c_138347768.htm.

33. La Chine, rivale céleste des États-Unis. [Online] Tribune de Genève, 01 06, 2019. https://www.tdg.ch/monde/chine-rivale-celeste-etatsunis/story/13604671.

34. Automatic Beijing-Zhangjiakou high-speed railway to open. [Online] CGTN, 10 29, 2019. https://news.cgtn.com/news/2019-10-28/Automatic-high-speed-railway-to-open-soon-L9DV9OpAXK/index.html.

35. Chinese cities with a population of 500,000 to have high-speed rail in 15 years. [Online] Chinadaily, 08 13, 2020. https://www.chinadaily.com.cn/a/202008/13/WS5f34ddfaa3108348172601d0.html.

36. China to build smart railway network by 2035 using 5G, BeiDou Navigation Satellite System. [Online] Globaltimes, 08 13, 2020. https://www.globaltimes.cn/content/1197628.shtml#:~:text=It%20said%20China%20will%20build,with%20population%20of%20over%20500%2C000..

37. China's high-speed railway network to double in length by 2035 under new blueprint. [Online] South China Morning Post, 08 14, 2020. https://www.scmp.com/economy/china-economy/article/3097226/china-high-speed-railway-network-double-length-2035-under.

38. Beijing is building hundreds of airports as millions of Chinese take to the skies. [Online] CNN, 05 26, 2019. https://edition.cnn.com/travel/article/china-new-airports/index.html#:~:text=World's%20largest%20aviation%20market&text=China%20currently%20has%20around%20235,across%20the%20country%20by%202035..

39. China forges ahead with airport construction binge, despite signs of slowing air traffic growth. [Online] South China Morning Post, 03 10, 2020. https://www.scmp.com/economy/china-economy/article/3074291/china-forges-ahead-airport-construction-binge-despite-signs.

40. SAIFEI - SAIFEI : une joint-venture dédiée au marché chinois. [Online] Safran-Group. https://www.safran-electrical-power.com/fr/societe/saifei.

41. Safran, partenaire majeur de COMAC, célèbre l'envol du C919. [Online] Safran-Group, 05 05, 2017. https://www.safran-group.com/fr/media/safran-partenaire-majeur-de-comac-celebre-lenvol-du-c919-20170505#:~:text=Safran%20est%20pr%C3%A9sent%20en%20Chine,chinoise%20comme%20AVIC%20et%20COMAC.&text=Safran%20occupe%2C%20seul%20ou%20en,ou%20europ%C3%A9en%20su.

42. Les réalisations de la Chine en matière de transport en chiffres. [Online] Peopledaily, 10 27, 2020. http://french.peopledaily.com.cn/Economie/n3/2020/1027/c31355-9773451.html.

43. Top 10 most valuable Chinese e-commerce companies. [Online] Chinadaily, 08 13, 2020. https://www.chinadaily.com.cn/a/202008/13/WS5f346fc0a31083481725fed2.html.

44. China home to 940 mln internet users : report. [Online] Xinhuanet, 09 29, 2020. http://www.xinhuanet.com/english/2020-09/29/c_139407651.htm.

45. Number of e-commerce users in China from 2017 to 2024. [Online] Statista.com. https://www.statista.com/forecasts/246032/e-commerce-users-in-china.

46. A 1000-Mile Long Clean Energy Artery Is Completed in China. [Online] Bloomberg, 06 04, 2020. https://www.bloomberg.com/news/articles/2020-06-04/china-state-grid-completes-3-17-billion-clean-power-uhv-line.

47. Wiedenbach, Annette. China Leads Green Jobs in Renewable Energy Sector. [Online] Climate Score Card, 09 26, 2020. https://www.climatescorecard.org/2020/09/china-leads-green-jobs-in-renewable-energy-sector/.

48. SCIO Briefing on 3rd Digital China Summit. [Online] China.org.cn, 09 22, 2020. http://www.china.org.cn/china/2020-09/22/content_76729591_3.htm.

49. China Focus : Multinational companies confident in China market. [Online] Xinhuanet, 10 22, 2019. http://www.xinhuanet.com/english/2019-10/22/c_138493756.htm.

50. General Motors Company's vehicle sales by key country in FY 2019. [Online] Statista.com, 02 12, 2020. https://www.statista.com/statistics/304367/vehicle-sales-of-general-motors-by-country/#:~:text=China%20was%20the%20largest%20single,the%20world's%20largest%20automobile%20market..

51. Pizza Hut Celebrates 30th Anniversary in China. [Online] Yum China Holding, 09 18, 2020. https://yumchinaholdingsinc.gcs-web.com/news-releases/news-release-details/pizza-hut-celebrates-30th-anniversary-china.

52. L'Union européenne et ses partenaires commerciaux. [Online] European Parliament. https://www.europarl.europa.eu/factsheets/fr/sheet/160/the-european-union-and-its-trade-partners.

53. La Chine devient le premier partenaire commercial de l'Europe. [Online] 24heures, 12 02, 2020. https://www.24heures.ch/la-chine-devient-le-premier-partenaire-commercial-de-leurope-311205073240.

54. China-Europe freight trains up 68% in July. [Online] CGTN, 08 09, 2020. https://news.cgtn.com/news/2020-08-09/China-Europe-freight-trains-up-68-in-July-SOBKSUtlMQ/index.html.

55. China-Europe freight train has completed more than 10,000 trips as of November. [Online] Globaltimes, 12 16, 2020. https://www.globaltimes.cn/content/1210102.shtml.

56. UBS puts economist on leave in growing China pig row. [Online] Reuters, 06 14, 2019. https://www.reuters.com/article/us-china-economy-politics-idUSKCN1TF0C8.

57. "Chinese pig" remark lands UBS in trouble as state firm excludes Swiss bank from bond sale. [Online] South China Morning Post, 06 17, 2019. https://www.scmp.com/business/banking-finance/article/3014843/chinese-pig-remark-lands-ubs-trouble-state-firm-excludes.

58. All the international brands that have apologized to China. [Online] supchina, 10 25, 2019. https://signal.supchina.com/all-the-international-brands-that-have-apologized-to-china/.

59. Lancôme Provokes Fury After Canceling a Concert in Hong Kong. [Online] New York Times, 06 07, 2016. https://www.nytimes.com/2016/06/08/business/international/lancome-hong-kong-denise-ho.html.

60. China's tiered city system explained. [Online] South China Morning Multimedia. https://multimedia.scmp.com/2016/cities/.

61. 宏观经济数据. [Online] Governement of Shouguang. http://www.shouguang.gov.cn/2020sssg/.

62. Comment Jinxiang est devenue la capitale chinoise de l'ail. [Online] Peopledaily, 10 25, 2017. http://french.peopledaily.com.cn/Economie/n3/2017/1025/c31355-9284589.html.

63. Population de nationalité étrangère. [Online] Swiss Confederation Administration, 12 22, 2020. https://www.bfs.admin.ch/bfs/fr/home/statistiques/population/migration-integration/nationalite-etrangere.html.

64. Religions. [Online] Swiss Confederation Administration, 12 22, 2020. https://www.bfs.admin.ch/bfs/fr/home/statistiques/population/langues-religions/religions.html.

65. Yu, Jinfeng. Trois façons de promouvoir le règlement unique des différends multiples. [Online] Chinacourt.org, 08 26, 2019. https://www.chinacourt.org/article/detail/2019/08/id/4397305.shtml.
66. Boncori, Anne-Laure and Brice, Lorraine. Ce que nous apprend le jeu de go sur la conduite des affaires. [Online] Haward Business Review France, 05 05, 2017. https://www.hbrfrance.fr/chroniques-experts/2017/05/15486-apprend-jeu-de-go-conduite-affaires/.
67. Why the China-EU investment deal is a long-term strategy for China. [Online] CGTN, 01 01, 2021. https://news.cgtn.com/news/2021-01-01/Why-the-China-EU-investment-deal-is-a-long-term-strategy-for-China-WGKwJBlGOQ/index.html.
68. What is China's 14th Five-Year Plan all about? [Online] CGTN, 11 07, 2020. https://news.cgtn.com/news/2020-11-07/What-is-China-s-14th-Five-Year-Plan-all-about--VdWpPn4CqI/index.html.
69. How Can Foreign Technology Investors Benefit from China's New Infrastructure Plan? [Online] China-briefing.com, 08 07, 2020. https://www.china-briefing.com/news/how-foreign-technology-investors-benefit-from-chinas-new-infrastructure-plan/#:~:text=In%20terms%20of%205G%20networks,in%20less%20than%20five%20years..